THE 7-POWER
CONTRACTOR^{SM}

RUN YOUR CONTRACTING BUSINESS
WITH LESS STRESS AND MORE SUCCESS^{SM}

AL LEVI

MY HOPE IS THAT YOUR READING THIS BOOK WILL GIVE YOU WHAT I ALWAYS WANTED, "LESS STRESS. MORE SUCCESS."

Al

APPLESEED BUSINESS, INC.
SCOTTSDALE, ARIZONA

Al Levi / Appleseed Business, Inc.
10632 N. Scottsdale Road, B-563
Scottsdale, AZ 85254
www.appleseedbusiness.com
info@appleseedbusiness.com

The 7-Power Contractor / Al Levi —1st ed.
ISBN 978-0-9972275-0-5

NOTICE TO READERS

To my wife, Natalie, and our daughters, Pamela and Jaclyn, who have supported me through thick and thin and encouraged me to share what I've learned.

To my brothers, Marty and Richie, and our Dad, Irving, the best business partners anyone could ever hope to have.

Contents

"It's only a real problem if time and money won't fix it."
—IRVING LEVI

Foreword

AS YOU OPEN THIS BOOK, it's best to understand one thing: Al's right. About everything he says. Because if Al doesn't know for sure about something, he won't weigh in. So when Al shares something, pay attention. He's right.

You may want to fuss, or argue, or question. Save yourself the trouble. Do what Al says. Buy yourself a bracelet that says "Do what Al says" to remind you so you don't waste any more time.

Want to have more success with less stress? Al can take you there. Need surefire systems and procedures? Al has written them. Want to make more money in less time? Al knows the way.

If more success with less stress is really what you are after, this book can help. Because what Al knows works.

In another man, Al's certainty might come across as arrogance. But with Al, it comes across as love. He doesn't need to share his wisdom. He has built a business and a fortune. Al is compelled to be of service because, once upon a time, he realized he was sacrificing his health and his relationships for the sake of his business. He knows what it's like to run on the treadmill of another day, another crazy situation.

Al and his family had built a mega-successful contracting business in Long Island, a tough union shop in a rough neighborhood. The money was good and the legacy was sound, but it was taking too big of a toll. Al wanted to leave and pursue other ventures, so he gave *three years notice*.

Al and his brothers systematized their processes, put together a solid plan, created operations manuals, and built a fully functioning training center, among other things. And it revolutionized their business.

Al did what so many owners want to do—build a company that runs without them, and create career opportunities for the team. In the process, he realized that his approach would work for others who were tired of the treadmill, and Appleseed Business Inc. was born.

I met Al Levi through a mutual friend, Dan Holohan. Al and I were involved in the same trade association and so I suggested we meet while at a convention. I was thinking we could hang out together for a few minutes between sessions. Al nailed me down for a specific time, and sent me an agenda for our conversation. Who does that? Al.

Twenty-five years later, Al has never once let me down. He inspires me with his insights, lessons, and friendship. If I were in trouble, I would call Al first. He has never been late for a phone call or a meeting. He is always prepared, and honors good procedure and business protocol. He is one of the best people I know, and he makes me better, too.

Al Levi is right. The right mentor, the right friend, and the right franchise partner. This book is filled with his wisdom. The keys to running your business with less stress and more success are recorded on its pages. Read on. Implement now. Your business and you too can be Al-right.

—Ellen Rohr, Small Business Expert, www.ellenrohr.com

[|]

Building a Dream, Not a Frankenstein

IS THERE A SHORTAGE of information out there on how to be successful in the contracting business? Nope!

There are plenty of great books, great trade associations, great online forum websites with active chat rooms, and a load of very talented industry consultants.

The problem is: How do you decide what information to listen to and how to make all the different information work together to get where you want to go?

These two issues come up again and again on the initial consulting calls I offer in my training and consulting business. These free 30-minute calls are a way for me to give back and honor all of the great mentors that have come into my life, not only for what they did for my business but also for helping me get my life headed in a better direction. If not for my mentors, I'd still be in a dark basement turning wrenches late into the evening!

That's right. Before I was a consultant, I was a contractor, just like you.

Visiting with you and others like you around the country, in big cities and little towns, and across a bunch of different trades, helps me keep my finger on the pulse of the contracting world and, in the process, spot new trends—good and bad.

INFORMATION OVERLOAD

One frightening trend I see is toward "contractor information overload," the result of the continuous consumption of business advice and information from too many different sources.

Let's face it. The Internet is one powerful tool for knowledge. But how do you know if you're talking to an expert or a knucklehead? (You don't!)

Even if you've been wise enough to get one-to-one consulting or join an industry education group or association, contractor overload is just a few taps away.

The problem is once you have that information, what do you do with it all? You're left wondering: Which thing gets done first? How do you get it in place at your company and keep it in place? Can you pull pieces of information from multiple places and make them all work together?

And then there's the question of what to do with that really good information that is downright contrary to other (supposedly) good information! One thing's for sure: everybody's got an opinion. Whether or not those opinions are truly useful is another story altogether.

BUILD A DREAM, NOT A FRANKENSTEIN

The negative effect of contractor overload became screamingly obvious to me after speaking with a contractor who said he was working with four different consultants and had been gathering advice from other consultants and industry groups for the *past 10 years!* He also wanted me to know that he was actively participating in an educational trade association.

My question to him was: "How is this approach working for you?"

He said, "We're speaking because it isn't working well at all and I know I'm still missing a lot of critical pieces, but I don't know where to go next."

I explained, "All the information and programs you now have don't necessarily go with one another because they were created apart from one another. You're busy building a 'Frankenstein!'"

Think of it this way: Would you put a Hemi engine in a Mini Cooper and expect it to perform properly? Assuming you could wedge all 426 cubic inches in there you'd be lucky to go 500 feet before the car shook apart, and if you did manage to get it going, you'd go deaf driving down the highway. The point is while they're both impressive individually in their own ways, combining them won't get you where you want to go because they are not designed to work together.

For example, we have specific scripts for customer service representatives and dispatchers that are not only in their procedure manuals but also integrated with the technician and other procedure manuals. So everything works *together.*

The key to overcoming contractor information overload is to find ways to filter effectively. But it's not always easy to discern the helpful information from the not helpful. This is actually a big problem because to build a dream instead of a Frankenstein, you'll need to make sure that whatever pieces you're pulling together will fit together perfectly. In other words, you need a *system.*

In fact, I'm betting one reason you are here is because you're hoping to find a total system for success that can be adapted to meet your needs *and* live up to your expectations.

Well, this book is designed to help you do just that.

THE 7-POWER CONTRACTOR: DEFINITION

A 7-Power Contractor is similar to being a five-tool player in baseball, an athlete who excels at hitting for average, hitting for power, base-running skills and speed, throwing ability, and fielding ability.

A 7-Power Contractor is a leader who is in command of the seven major areas that require their attention as an owner—leadership and planning, operations, finance, selling, marketing, staffing, and sales coaching.

The good news is becoming a 7-Power Contractor is not nearly as hard as becoming a five-tool baseball player. All that is required is a desire to succeed, a commitment to getting organized, and a willingness to follow the program.

WRITTEN BY CONTRACTORS, FOR CONTRACTORS

The contents of this book come directly from people who know what is required to succeed not only because we have achieved success ourselves, but also because we've helped thousands of other contractors run their businesses with more success and less stress. I was raised in my family's plumbing, heating, and cooling business and it was my desire to leave the business—*without* leaving my two brothers and my dad in the lurch—that drove me to figure all of this out, and focus full time on teaching others what I had learned, the basics of which are outlined in this book.

Over the past 20 years, I've taught these concepts to contractors in a dozen or more industries—plumbing, heating, cooling, electrical, cabinetry, handyman, condominium building, roofing, home insulation, and even photography—so I know that if you work at them, they will work for you, too.

That said, to make it easier to trust the information you're getting here, I thought it might help to hear it from someone else who is like you, has tried it before, and has had success.

That's why I've invited a few of my clients to share their stories—the good, the bad, and the formerly ugly. All agreed to participate because they want you to know you can trust what you will learn here has value, and it can work for you, too.

Together we'll show you the path to building the dream company you've always imagined. We're happy you're here.

Let's begin. (No more Frankenstein.)

The 7 Powers

THE 7 POWERS are Planning Power, Operations Power, Financial Power, Staffing Power, Marketing Power, Sales Power, and Sales Coaching Power, and they're designed to work *together*. Planning Power, however, is always on and running in the background, kind of like the operating system on your computer.

PLANNING POWER

Planning Power, in a nutshell, is the ability to set a goal and then confidently and consistently work on the right things, at the right time, in the right way to make that goal a reality.

Planning Power will stabilize your situation and provide you with the structures and direction you need to leverage the six other powers. In this system, Planning Power should always be undertaken first. *No exceptions.* If you don't know where you're going, you're going to end up someplace else!

Planning Power is always on because planning is what drives all the elements of the other powers forward, like an engine. Once the basics are pinned down and the projects are humming along, Planning Power falls in love and marries Leadership Power, and then you really start to go places—fast!

We start with Planning Power because it will get you out of the ocean and safely back in the boat and motoring forward. The addition of Leadership Power provides the focus, commitment, and energy needed to raise and trim the sails so that the boat can get you where you want to go faster.

Don't worry, we will connect Planning Power to Leadership Power for you at the end of the book. Planning Power is first because the best sails in the world won't be able to move you forward until they are attached to the mast of a seaworthy vessel.

OPERATING POWER

Next up is Operating Power. This critical power is undertaken second, again no exceptions. Operating Power is manifested through the creation of policies and procedures for every task, in every department of your company, and the implementation of systems that will enable the company to run systematically and automatically without you from day to day. By creating written documentation about what people need to know when they need to know it, you may even begin to look forward to sharing the knowledge that you used to keep to yourself because you know each thing you transfer to the page is one less thing you have to do yourself!

FINANCIAL POWER

The next power we suggest you tackle is Financial Power. Financial Power is expressed through a known financial position (KFP) and accurate selling prices that are driven by your budget, not the market. You also need to know the difference between tax accounting and the kind of accounting you do to make sure your business stays on track day to day. To achieve your goals, you need to take control of your financials and monitor them weekly. Yes, weekly. (We'll provide you with a fast budget and pricing model you can use to get your prices in the ballpark. Key word: ballpark. Ellen Rohr's self-study materials are excellent and will lead you through step by step.)

STAFFING POWER

The next power in line is Staffing Power. Staffing Power comes from your commitment to constantly recruit people with the right attitude and develop them in-house, with continuous and comprehensive training. Staffing Power also puts an end to awkward end-of-day "Got a minute?" meetings with employees who want to ask you for a raise.

Staffing power ensures everyone will know what the next level is, how much it pays, and exactly what they need to do to get there. When you have this power, you are helping existing staff get better and encouraging those who don't want to play a better game to go work for your competitors!

SELLING POWER

Selling Power focuses on the selling process, specifically on how each employee affects the selling process. Few if any of us are "born to sell," but there are a multitude of ways that anyone can get better, if they really want to get better, starting with thoroughly documented procedures (remember Operating Power?) and continuous training (Staffing Power).

Are you beginning to get the picture? All the powers are integrated and reinforce each other. No Frankenstein!

Once the selling price has been established through Financial Power, the number of clients you can service well has been determined through Staffing Power, and the tools to sell have been given through Selling Power, you can begin to undertake Marketing Power.

MARKETING POWER

Marketing Power ensures we are marketing in a way that will effectively reach our target audience—those most likely to desire what we're selling and who are more than willing to pay for our expertise and professionalism.

In fact, Marketing Power is as much about demonstrating our professionalism at every juncture as it is about letting prospective customers know we are out there. Marketing Power ensures that every encounter customers have with our company reinforces an image of professionalism, from our logos to our trucks, forms, business cards, uniforms, and shoe covers, and even how we greet the customer at the door.

SALES COACHING POWER

It should come as no surprise that the final power, Sales Coaching Power, and Selling Power are linked. Selling Power is about the system of selling, while Sales Coaching Power is all about measuring the selling results and creating a reward system that *rewards the right stuff.*

You'll want to make sure you have Financial Power before you start Sales Coaching Power, because one of the beautiful things about this system is that it is designed to reward people with *money they create!* (And if they aren't creating any money, we'll tell you how you can deal with that as well.)

Now that you have the 30,000-foot view of all seven powers, and how they influence and empower each other, let's get this show on the road.

Next stop: Planning Power.

[|]

Planning Power

IF YOU'RE LIKE MOST contractors, you probably spend the majority of your day putting out the fires that your company set yesterday, with the knowledge that the fires you put out today are bound to pop up again tomorrow. And here's the bad news—this pattern is going to continue until you change the way you spend your week.

How do I know? I did exactly the same thing for years at my own company.

What changed this destructive pattern? I got sick of it!

I was lucky enough to have a good-sized company where there were people other than me to work on things and deliver the products and services our company sold. The problem was that I had a stranglehold on too many things, so even though there were other hands that could potentially help me, I didn't let them.

The staff always seemed busy already so I didn't want to overburden them, but I didn't want to keep killing myself either. So one day, I mustered the courage to ask the staff members to bring the projects they were currently working on into the conference room. Once everyone was inside, I asked them to dump what they brought on the conference table.

To my horror, many people were working on projects that they felt I had made a priority but I actually didn't even know they were working on. And worse yet, there were two or more staff members working on the same project independently, so they were headed off in different directions.

It was a sickening, but vitally important, learning moment for all.

RIGHT THINGS, RIGHT TIME, RIGHT WAY

To fix this problem—and ensure we were working on the right things, at the right time, in the right way—we decided to write out one list of all the projects in progress. We then discussed and added to the list the projects and habits we felt we should be working on in the next year or so.

Projects were things like exiting the warehouse, operations manuals, and Staffing Power. Habits were patterns of behavior we wanted to establish, e.g., steps of delegation, time tracking, and corrective action.

We called this big fat list of about 100 items our master project list.

There was no way we could tackle everything at once, so we had to filter it down to concentrate our mental and financial firepower. We boiled the list down to the projects and habits we needed to get in place based on two filters:

the project or habit had to either solve our biggest problem or challenge, or give us the greatest chance to grow and be profitable in the coming year. Using these two criteria, we culled the list down to 30 items, which we called—you guessed it—our top 30 list.

The idea of tackling that many initiatives was still too daunting, so we ran each project through the filtering process again to identify the top five projects or habits we thought would make the biggest positive impact at our company, which we called—predictably—our top five list.

Note: it will be tempting to jump directly to your top five projects, but it's only by methodically filtering all the projects that you will be able to arrive at the right five projects, as well as identify and load up 25 other "right" projects to accomplish over a one-year period.

THE TOP FIVE LIST

Once we had the top five list, we created a chart with three columns across the top:

- **Column One**: What we need. This is where we defined exactly what it is we need. The top five item.
- **Column Two**: Why we need it. This is where we justified the importance of doing this project.
- **Column Three**: Status. This was our way of tracking the progress and feedback on the project's priority.

We then posted this matrix on a whiteboard, where everyone in the company would see it. We knew if we posted the list in a prominent place there would be a higher level of accountability and ownership.

Rolling out the Top Five Whiteboard

Below is the template my clients use for rolling out their top five whiteboard:

- **Step One**: Hang the whiteboard in a prominent place where everyone will see it each day.
- **Step Two**: Call the whole team together to let them know what this board is all about. Company owners and top management should be smiling and exuding excitement as they greet the staff. Then you (the owner) need to say something like this: "We know in the past we've rolled out programs too fast, without enough thinking behind them and without enough of your input. For that, I hope you will accept our heartfelt apologies. What you see on this whiteboard are the company's top five projects. It was a hard process to choose just five. But the key thing for you to know is that we as owners and managers are committed to having us as a team working on the right thing, at the right time, in the right way. And that's why we're all excited to be here with you today to share the great news!"
- **Step Three**: You and your team then need to start spending a part of each week working on your top five priorities, *so they get done!*

It's called working on the right things, at the right time, in the right way. And it works.

Start building your own big list of all the projects that you and your company need to complete, and work on advancing the items on your top five list each week. Then watch how fast your company gets better!

Note: To see some examples of top five white boards be sure to download your Bonus Materials using the link and password on "Bonus Materials" page at the end of this book.

TOP FIVE LIST LESSONS — MARK PAUP

The top 30 and top five project lists are what took us from an average company to a great company.

Let me give you an example. Originally, the name of our company was City Rule Plumbing, Heating, and Cooling. The problem was that there was another company in town that was called City-Wide Heating and Air Conditioning. When we advertised, people would say, "Oh, you're the green truck guys," and we said, "No, we're City Rule."

The only way to fix this problem was to change the company name, so we moved that project to the top of our top five list.

The name change meant all the branded items throughout the company needed to be redone with the new logo and colors—invoices, shirts, trucks, you name it. We got it all done in three months. Nobody confuses us with the green truck guys anymore. When you see us and you hear us, you know it's Golden Rule.

Without the top five list to focus us, we would have done a couple of trucks, then we would have waited until it felt right to do more. We might have done shirts. We would have finished stuff when we thought about it, or slowed down.

*We work on our top five projects all through the year now, in-
stead of whenever it's convenient, and that's the difference
maker.*

—Mark Paup, President, Golden Rule Plumbing,
Heating and Cooling, Grimes, Iowa

AL'S MEETING MANIFESTO

Many of the items on your top five list will require a group
effort, which means that to stay in sync and on track you'll
need to communicate with each other.

The best way to do this is not by e-mail. (Or worse, text
message.) It is by getting those responsible together in a
room (whether in a physical space or virtually using a web-
based tool such as GoToMeeting or Join.me) for a productive discussion.

In fact, meetings are the most effective way to communicate with your team and are actually a very efficient
use of everyone's time—when done properly.

Here are 10 guidelines you can use to make sure your
meetings make the most of everyone's time and attention:

1. Every meeting must have a meeting coach. A meet-
    ing coach's job is to keep things moving, and ensure
    all agenda items are addressed and the meeting
    ends on time.
2. All meetings must have a written agenda.
3. Someone other than the meeting coach should take
    notes and write a summary report.

4. Meetings should have definite beginning and end times. If someone is late one time, that is forgiven. If they are late again, they are banned from entering the meeting in progress. Meetings end on time. No exceptions.

5. The fewer people at the meeting, the better.

6. Meetings cover items on the written agenda only. Any items outside of the agenda are recorded and put on the agenda for the next meeting.

7. Meetings are sacred and not to be disturbed unless absolutely necessary.

8. Shorter, more frequent meetings are better than longer meetings held less frequently because you will more easily sustain people's attention.

9. A round table or tight square table will increase equality and promote better listening.

10. A well-appointed meeting room, with comfortable chairs, good lighting, and multimedia items such as a TV, whiteboard, flip chart, and Internet access will maximize potential for productive meetings.

RUNNING MEETINGS – KATHY BETLEM

We have a meeting every week now for service, install, sales, customer service representatives, dispatchers, and leadership, and sometimes the staff will say to me, "Really? All these meetings?" But you know what? I would be lost if I missed my meetings because they help me keep a handle on everything that's going on.

For example, in the morning service meeting, the techs will tell me what is happening on the calls so in my afternoon meeting I can tell the CSRs what we need to work on. One meeting leads to the other, and it's all about what's going on and keeping everybody on the same page.

We follow Al's meeting guidelines. We have a written agenda. We have a person taking notes. We give out the agenda the day before and we stay on topic. I posted the guidelines in our meeting rooms at first so that we could go down the list and make sure that we were sticking to them.

The other thing is we start on time. The door gets closed. And if that door's closed, you cannot come in. Let me tell you, I don't have people missing meetings. They are there prior to that door being closed. It's very funny. They're running because they know I'll shut the door on them. I'm always like, "Seriously, you guys?" But the important thing is they are there and they are there on time.

—Kathy Betlem, Vice President, John Betlem Heating and Cooling, Rochester, New York

PLANNING POWER: PEARLS

- Work on the right things, at the right time, in the right way.
- Create a master project list and then whittle it down to the 30 projects and habits that will either solve your biggest problem or challenge, or give you the

greatest chance to grow and be profitable in the coming year.

- Apply the criteria mentioned above again to your top 30 list to arrive at your top five list of projects and habits to focus on now. When you finish one top five project, pull one up from your top 30 list.
- Post the top five list on a whiteboard where everyone can see it.
- Stay on top of your top five projects by holding meetings using Al's Meeting Manifesto.

[|]

Operating Power

ARE YOU THE ONLY ONE who really knows what's going on at your shop? The only one who gets to go to the trade-group meetings, workshops, and training sessions? Do you work in secrecy, keeping your staff in the dark about why you're doing the things you're doing?

If you answered yes, you might be a knowledge pig!

KNOWLEDGE PIG SYNDROME

A knowledge pig is someone who hogs all the knowledge. It's not always intentional. Have you ever run a marketing campaign or sales special but neglected to inform the company? Or run a help-wanted ad but forgot to tell the people who answer the phone? (It happens a lot more than you can imagine.)

I don't think you're sloppy or doing any of this on purpose. Somewhere along the line you got some (bad) advice that said keeping staff in the dark helps you retain control, when actually it does just the opposite. When employees are kept in the dark, they will be consistently inconsistent because they don't know all that they should know to do their jobs effectively!

THREE LITTLE OWNER IDENTITIES

Business owners can slide into knowledge pigdom when too much of their identity is wrapped up in their business. Even though they may also be described as a parent, spouse, member of a local organization, bowler, etc., much of who they are is invested in who they are *at work*.

See if you identify with any of these profiles:

- **The Guru Pig**: "I'm the only one here who really knows the ins and outs of this business. I cringe to think what their work would look like if they didn't check with me first."
- **The Rescuer Pig**: "I feel like I have to help every employee with every simple task. I don't know how these people manage to get up in the morning without me!"
- **The Fireman Pig**: "This place would fall apart without me. I can't even take my family on vacation for a few days for fear that the place would burn down without me there to put out the fire."

Seeing yourself as the glue that is holding your company together might make you feel better, even rather important. People depend on you to lead the way, to take control, to share your knowledge. Without you, there wouldn't be a company!

Underneath all of this, however, is the real reason you don't want to share your knowledge, one so scary that no one ever mentions it.

I'm talking about fear.

Fear is the little voice inside you that says, "I'm afraid to pass on all of my knowledge. If I do, then they might not need me anymore. And if that happens, then *who am I?*"

Fear is the reason we resist documenting our knowledge and teaching it to others. We stop just short of passing it on, so we don't have to let go of any power and lose our identity.

The problem with this way of thinking is that employees can only act on the limited knowledge they have, and since their knowledge is incomplete, they can't help but disappoint you.

Without your knowledge and clear direction on what you expect them to do with that knowledge, employees will need to rely on *their* common sense and *their* interpretation of what needs to be done and how to do it, and it will never be the same as yours.

The bottom line is this: without others at your company knowing what you know, the company can't grow, and that ultimately will translate into less success and more stress for you.

So, if your goal truly is to gain control of your company and your life, then it's time to start sharing some of that knowledge, and with it, some of the responsibility for using it, too.

The good news is that what I've found at most companies is the staff is more than anxious to learn something new and something of value. They want to get smarter, they want to do a good job, and most of all they want a voice in the decision-making. Sharing your knowledge instead of hogging it not only helps ensure employee buy-in, it also makes work a lot more rewarding for them, and for you, too.

BUILD IT ONCE – GAROLD GIPMAN

Through Planning Power, we were able to simplify our whole operation—a lot. We set up what we needed to run the company and created an organizational chart. Then we took each operation back to the basics and broke everything down to key steps.

Before we wrote everything down in the operations manuals, nobody really knew what they were doing. It was like, "OK, do this random thing today." Once we got organized, we realized we could do the same amount of work with four fewer employees!

One of our biggest problems was that we were constantly having product come back for rework. A wrong stain color would go on a door, or a countertop would get cut wrong. Most cabinet companies build their own cabinets and order in their doors and countertops. We build our own cabinets, but we also build our own doors, manufacture our own counter-

tops, and do all of our own finishing. Keeping all four working harmoniously is a challenge!

Between the production meetings, daily huddles, and the operations manuals, now everybody knows exactly how we are building something in the shop. We're more productive than ever and there's been almost no rework. It's amazing.

—Garold Gipman, General Manager, Gipman Millwork and
Design, Cranbrook, British Columbia

SYSTEMS TO GO

Once you've decided to share what you know, the next step is to create and implement systems around that knowledge and provide staff with the documentation needed to allow the company to run systematically and automatically from day to day *without you.*

Systems can make any company run better and be more profitable. They can help you have explosive and manageable growth during the good times and provide stability when you're struggling through slow times. In fact, the best companies I work with actually grow during a recession because they're in a position to benefit from all the competition that falls away when things get tough.

By systems, I mean policies and procedures that detail how everything in your company should be done, from paying bills, entering invoices, answering calls, and dispatching to having your trucks set up the right way and training people to excel. Systems also apply to budgeting and other financial metrics that help you know where you are at any minute financially. There are also a lot of systems that must be in place for accounts receivable, accounts payable, and human resources—not to mention how the actual customer is treated and how the work gets done!

If five very skilled and talented technicians started working for you tomorrow, what are the chances they could go straight into the field and perform exactly to your company's specifications?

If the chances are slim to none, then you should begin building your operations manual without delay. The lack of defined procedures could be rendering your employees helpless, or worse, causing them to deliver inconsistent service to your customers.

Just like a restaurant must be able to take orders right, cook meals right, and clear tables quickly when it's a crazy busy Saturday night, contractors must be able to answer phones the right way when they are ringing off the hook, dispatch in a way that maximizes techs' talents, and ensure that techs in the field are thoroughly trained with great sales, operational, and technical skills when they show up on a customer's doorstep.

An operations manual will also help you determine the current skill levels and technical knowledge of your more "experienced" employees. You may be surprised to find out how much they do not know!

As you begin to create and document these systems, keep in mind the following guidelines:

- **Done = 80 Percent**: Written policies and procedures should be created for every task in every department of the company, but they will never cover 100 percent of what you do. Your goal is to cover the 80 percent of what goes on in the day to day so that you and your team are free to handle the 20 percent of the out of the ordinary (i.e., the weird).

- **Don't Expect to Love It:** If you're like most of my clients, you will find the process of writing down everything you do and exactly how to do it the most tedious thing you have done since learning your times tables. I know. I have been there. Not only did I do it for my family's contracting business, I also worked next to many a consulting client as they filled out their documents, encouraging them and coaching them toward that 80 percent goal.

- **Hire Help if You Need It:** If it's just too painful, you may want to consider hiring a writer to help you to get the knowledge out of your head and onto the page.

Whatever your approach, I urge you to make a decision right now to do it. Creating these documents and making them available to employees in a comprehensive operations manual is a critical beginning step toward running your business with less stress and more success.

OPERATION CONFIDENCE – MARK PAUP

We set up a manual for each position so that when we hire somebody now, they have an exact description of what their job is and how to do it. That way, when employees run across something they aren't sure of, they can refer back to the manual and figure it out, rather than going to their manager with basic questions like, "How do I enter this invoice," or "How do I close out this call?" We can just direct them back to the manual and they can figure it out. It saves a lot of time.

For the service technicians, we created operation-specific manuals that have step-by-step directions for how to do most of what they will run into in the field. The manual is the technician's backup, but it is also their confidence because if they get out on the job and have questions, they can always refer back to it.

This is huge because in our industry it's all about confidence. Before we made the manual, techs were constantly calling their field supervisor to ask, "Is this right?" The problem is that makes it harder for the field supervisor to do his job because he's answering these silly questions all day long. The operation-specific manual helps both of them do their jobs better.

—Mark Paup, President, Golden Rule Plumbing,
Heating and Cooling, Grimes, Iowa

YOU ARE RESPONSIBLE

The bottom line is this: as an employer, the burden of responsibility for your employees' levels of competence, or incompetence, ultimately falls on you.

That's right . . . on *you* . . . not them!

In addition, the increasingly stringent regulations and liability in the contracting industry demand that your technicians follow proper procedure. If you do not have a policy and procedure for every task your company performs, then you are essentially telling your employees to "do what you want, however you want."

With an operations manual, you can insist that your employees play by the company rulebook. You have every right to run your company your way. Your operations manual will help you to be fair in the process.

Building the policies and procedures that go in the operations manual can be a little tedious, but it's not difficult. It's a matter of methodically walking through every step until you've fully documented the experience you want the customer to have.

To get a feel for this, grab a piece of paper and write down the first five steps for the following activities at your company:

- Answering the phone (customer service representative)
- Greeting the customer at the door (service technician)
- Preparing and presenting a proposal (systems engineer, or "big-ticket" salesperson)

You get the idea. The next step is to do this *for every single activity in your company.*

Once the policies and procedures are completed and added to the operations manual, all new policies and procedures should include an employee sign-off sheet to ensure that the revised or new policy or procedure has been read and understood. Do your best to ensure that affected employees have an opportunity to contribute their feedback before a new procedure is issued. Many times it's the people doing the job every day who have the best ideas on how to improve a particular procedure.

Sometimes clients are under the impression they already have an operations manual but nine times out of 10 what they actually have is an *employee* manual. An employee manual contains your code of ethics and documents your expectation of how employees should behave, so it should be a section in the operations manual. Most of your operations manual, however, will be devoted to the description of exactly how you expect your employees to *do their job*.

EMPOWERING THE PROCESS

Once the manuals are completed, you will need to activate them over time, through a series of structured meetings and a spirit of communication similar to the one you made when you rolled out the top five whiteboard.

Important: Since you will be making a big deal about how things are really changing this time, do not include any policy or procedure in the operations manual you are not willing to create training systems to support, or you are not willing to enforce consistently.

Systems, policies, procedures, and manuals can only be as effective as the level of commitment you have to following through and sticking to the program yourself.

Note: A sample chapter of an operations manual is included in your Bonus Materials, which you can download using the link and password on the "Bonus Materials" page at the end of this book.

OPERATING POWER: PEARLS

- Don't be a knowledge pig. Share what you know so your employees know what they need to do their job right.

- Systems, policies, and procedures will free you to look after the weird stuff and keep you from having to rush in and save the day, day after day after day.

- When it comes to documenting procedures, 80 percent = done.

- You don't have to love it, but to be successful, the documentation of processes, systems, procedures, and policies must occur. Hire a technical writer to help, if needed.

- Ultimately, you are responsible and the program will only be as effective as your commitment to follow through on it.

- Don't implement anything you're not prepared to back up with training systems and full enforcement.

[|]

Financial Power

WHAT TO CHARGE per hour is by far the question people ask most frequently on their free 30-minute consulting calls. The first question I ask them is whether they are currently doing budgeting on a regular basis at their business.

More often than not, the answer is no.

How Much Should I Charge?

Most of the contractors I talk to are basing their current per hour rate on what they believe their market can bear.

This number is usually based on guerrilla research such as calling around anonymously and asking what competitors charge by the hour. Or they are trying to figure out who they're losing bids to based on pricing, and working backward to figure out that company's hourly rate.

A few admit that they talk to their competitors and compare notes about pricing. The only problem with this research tactic, in case you're not aware of it, is that it is illegal. The other name for it is *price fixing*.

Regardless of how you're pricing—time and materials or, better yet, flat rate—budgeting is the only way to arrive at what your hourly price really should be.

Small business and financial expert Ellen Rohr says it is foolhardy to base your hourly rate on what your competitors are charging because they might be on the fast track to going broke!

In her book titled How Much Should I Charge?: Pricing Basics for Making Money Doing What You Love, Ellen teaches that you need to charge for all of what it costs to be in business and build in the profit you wish to make.

Let me repeat that. *You need to charge for all of what it costs to be in business and build in the profit you wish to make.*

The problem is that we, as contractors, often are only accounting for the hourly salary we pay our technicians and the cost of materials and equipment without factoring in all the other overhead costs associated with running a business that is built to last.

THE CUSTOMER PAYS FOR EVERYTHING

Callers are also surprised when I tell them that charging the right price ultimately is in the customer's best interest.

Yes, your customers, like you, all like a good price. But even more than that, they want the peace of mind that comes with knowing you, the contractor, are going to do the job right the first time, and stand behind your work should a problem arise.

If you don't charge enough, you'll struggle to stay in business and that financial pressure will force you to make decisions that ultimately are in the best interest of *no one*, because you won't take care of the customer the way they deserve, much less in a way that will keep them coming back and singing your praises to their friends and family.

Think about it. If you don't charge enough, how will you be able to afford to absorb the cost of running a callback when it arises? Attract and keep good staff? Invest in the latest technology? Provide your staff with ongoing training?

How comfortable would you be adjusting a gas-fired piece of equipment and then not doing a carbon monoxide test? (I hope not very comfortable.)

How comfortable would you be clearing a sewer line and then not putting a camera in the line to verify that the blockage is fully removed and there's no obstruction, collapse, roots, sand, or other bigger issue that still needs attention?

I hope not comfortable *at all*.

In fact, it was the great Frank Blau Jr. who once told me, "The customer pays for everything because it's in their best interest to do so."

Want to better understand why you need to do budgeting and charge a properly arrived at hourly rate so that you can calculate the appropriate flat rate for your services? Pricing that takes into consideration what you should be charging based on what you need to not only provide top-notch services but also make the amount of profit you need and want to make?

Good. Below is an exercise that can at least help get you in the ballpark. Let me be clear here. This is *not* a replacement for a full-blown budgeting process and other financial work, but it *is* a quick way to better understand what it takes to be in business.

FAST BUDGET AND PRICING

COLUMN ONE

For column one you will need a list of all your year-end expenses from your accountant. Look at each of those expenses and determine as best as you can what the additional costs for each could be in the year ahead. For example, maybe the cost of vehicle insurance is going up. Or your medical coverage costs are increasing. Or maybe rent and utilities at your shop will cost more. Column one is a list of all it took to be in business last year, plus your best guess at what additional costs there will be for these items in the coming year.

COLUMN TWO

Column two is a list of what you plan to do differently in the year ahead to advance your business toward the goals you've set for the coming year and beyond, and what you think each will cost. For example, you want or need to do more marketing to get more calls from the customers to avoid a steep drop-off in work. Add paid weekly meetings to improve communications. Or invest in ongoing training classes beyond just weekly meetings. Or improve the technology at your company, such as phones, tablets, computers, and more.

Add columns one and two together. This is your new breakeven number. But wait, there's more.

COLUMN THREE

Column three is where you put down the amount of profit you desire. That's right. You actually have to *decide* how much profit you want to make.

We're not in business to lose money. And we're not in business to just break even, either. We're in business to make money because when we do, it benefits the customers, the company, and all who work at the company, including the owners.

OK, let's put some numbers to this:

Column one:	$900,000
Column two:	$100,000
Total of above:	$1,000,000
Add your desired profit:	$200,000
Total budgeted gross sales:	$1,200,000

Let's say you have six technicians at your company. You would divide that $1,200,000 by six. That tells you that to reach your goal, each tech will need to bring in $200,000 in sales this year.

If each technician works 50 weeks a year at 40 hours a week with no overtime, they work 2,000 hours in a year. Traditionally, technicians are 50 percent efficient, which means you pay them for eight hours but they actually only bill out and work four hours. Still, each technician will give you 1,000 billable hours a year.

You now have a total of 6,000 billable hours to sell to generate $1,200,000 of profitable sales. Divide $1,200,000 by 6,000 and you arrive at an hourly selling price of $200 per hour.

Eye opening ... isn't it?

My goal here, as it is in all my 30-minute consulting calls, is to share some business basics. What you do about it is always your decision. My hope here is that you do your financial homework and commit to doing real budgeting at your company on a regular basis and find out what the right selling price at your company should be.

Note: A Fast Budget spreadsheet has been provided in the Bonus Materials, which you can download using the link and password on the "Bonus Materials" page at the end of this book

KEEP IT REAL WORLD ACCOUNTING

There's a big difference between the tax accounting your accountant does for you and "real-world" accounting, which is the type of accounting you need to do to make sound financial decisions about your business, says our financial expert, Ellen Rohr. She explains here:

"Tax accounting done by your accountant is designed to either delay the payment of taxes or to minimize the taxes you legitimately need to pay—both very good things. Using tax documents to make financial business decisions, however, is like driving your financial car by looking in the rear-view mirror.

"Real-world accounting is based on operating from a known financial position (KFP). Your company might already be there, or you may have some work to do. A KFP means your books are all up to date, as is your P/L (profit/loss) statement and balance sheet. You know what you owe and who owes you what, and you know what's coming in, what's going out, and when, among other things.

"Once you are at a KFP, then real-world accounting is about consistently using certain tools that will assist you in making the best possible financial decisions for your business."

Ellen recommends that you check in on your financial status weekly. That's right, every week by doing a financial quick check (FQC for short). In an FQC, you take a look at your income, expenses, payroll, and cash flow ratio.

The FQC is a spreadsheet that tells you how much you've sold, in what categories, what you've spent in direct costs, and your operating expenses. It also tells your gross margin and net profit, and what your cash flow is.

Based on that information, you can make proactive decisions about the business that you think will improve your position.

By doing this religiously every week, you will find that you are able to uncover potential problems and take action to remedy them much earlier, and, if not eliminate financial surprises, at least see some of them coming!

As soon as you're ready to fully develop your financial power, I highly recommend you take advantage of Ellen's excellent self-study materials available on her website, which is listed on the resource page at the end of this book.

KNOW THE SCORE – MARK PAUP

I used to look at my bank statements at the end of the month and see if I had more deposits than debts, and that's how I determined if I was making money or not. To look back at it now, it's just so crazy I can't even believe it.

I played football, so I always compare it to a football game. Could you imagine playing quarter one and having no idea what the score is? Then you go to halftime and you're trying to give your pep talk, but you still have no idea what the score is. Then you get down to the fourth quarter and you find out you're down 21 points.

Well, what changes are you going to be able to make in the fourth quarter of a game—or the fourth week of a month—to really make an impact? You're probably not going to be able to make up that drastic of a loss. The ability to make decisions as you go along, like a coach does in the first quarter or at halftime, is the key to managing your financials. Every month is a game, and every month you want to win.

All our spending decisions are now made based on our financials—our balance sheet, P/L, and the financial quick check. It's a big mental shift. I used to think, "Well, we're in business, it'll come from somewhere," and that's just completely the wrong attitude.

I make much better business decisions now because I know what my numbers are and what they mean.

—Mark Paup, President, Golden Rule Plumbing, Heating and Cooling, Grimes, Iowa

REMINDER

Financial management and marketing are the two responsibilities that *must always remain with you*, the owner. If you completely delegate the financial role, you may find yourself out of the loop with what is really going on with your company financially, with potentially disastrous results. If you abdicate responsibility for marketing, without your vision there's no guarantee that your company will be represented to customers the way you want and need it to be.

Remember: the responsibility for your company's financials and marketing can never be relinquished.

FINANCIAL POWER: PEARLS

- Don't base your hourly rate on what you think the market will bear or what your competitors are charging. They could be going broke!
- You need to charge for all of what it costs to be in business and the profit you wish to make. To know what that number is you have to create a budget.
- "The customer pays for everything because it's in their best interest to do so." — Frank Blau Jr.
- Use real-world accounting to run your business, not tax accounting.

- Get to a known financial position and monitor your finances weekly with a financial quick check.
- Financial management is one of two roles at your company (the other being marketing) that you are always responsible for.

Staffing Power

YOU'VE FINALLY MADE IT BACK to your office after another crazy day. Just as you plop down into your chair to
begin digging through the pile of stuff that has been hap-
hazardly dumped on your desk by your staff, there's a knock
at your door. Usually, it'll be around five o'clock. At least,
that's when it would happen to me.

THE FIVE-O'CLOCK KNOCK

You look up from your desk, and see one of your employees
(let's call him Bob) standing in your doorway. Bob says,
"Hey, boss, you got a minute? Because we need to talk."

You feel your body tighten up because you instinctively
know what's coming next (and it's not good). Bob's either
here to give you the "I need a raise" ultimatum, or to tell you
that he has taken another job.

Here's the thing: by the time the employee appears in
your doorway, nine times out of 10 you either will need to

buy back their allegiance to keep them on or start looking for their replacement because it will be too late to save them.

If it's another job, it means Bob has probably been planning to leave for some time, and all you can do at this point is make a hard sell to try and keep him on.

If Bob is threatening to leave unless you raise his pay, that's another problem with another set of implications entirely.

THE RAISE-MY-SALARY GAME

You can choose to play along with the "raise-my-salary game" and you may end up saving Bob—for a while. The problem is this: it leaves the door wide open for everyone else who works for you to come in and renegotiate his or her pay, too.

Every time you do capitulate, you will feel taken advantage of, and the employee also will go away worse for the experience because he or she will feel like a kid fighting for an increase in allowance. Rarely do these hard feelings subside for either party. In fact, it usually only postpones the inevitable, and no one wins.

STAFFING STEPS

I decided the only way to permanently minimize the chances of being surprised by an employee and the plans they had for my company (and me) was to begin living by this motto: "Always be recruiting, hiring, orienting, training, and retaining."

In fact, after working with hundreds of clients, what I can tell you is this: without ongoing, aggressive, and never-ending efforts in those five areas, it will be very tough to build the kind of company you dreamed of when you first got into the contracting business. To do that, your organization must be filled with "right stuff" people.

The best way to address this issue is to create career paths that are clearly defined in writing.

Before you can create these career paths, however, you need to know how your company is structured and how each person in it contributes to its success. You need an organizational chart.

THE ORGANIZATIONAL CHART

All businesses are composed of a number of distinct roles, even if there is only one person doing (or not doing) all of them. An organizational chart paints a clear picture of all the different roles that are necessary to run your business successfully, and provides a foundation for making decisions about who (else) needs to be in those roles—even if your name is now the only one in the majority of the boxes.

Your organizational chart is also a critical first step in mapping out exactly how employees can grow within your company.

Contrary to popular belief, an organizational chart is not about rank or prestige. It is a visual aid that enables you to understand exactly who is responsible for what, and who their backup is. As your company grows, people you train or hire will take your place in many of those roles, so you can spend more of your day *leading* your business rather than working in it!

Once the career paths are clearly defined in writing, the next step is to establish performance-based salary levels (i.e., salary ladders).

It's the only fair way to do it.

In this model, pay is tied to demonstrated performance, and it is a real blessing to owners and employees alike. The great thing is it takes you both out of the salary tug-of-war. Remember five-o'clock knock Bob? Under this system, Bob would know exactly how to get his own raise in pay.

In fact, this system works so well that many of my clients use it during the recruiting and hiring process. They do this because they know it sets them apart from their competitors, and the "right stuff" people are attracted to companies who think ahead and provide a concrete career path versus just a job.

ORGANIZING THE ORGANIZATION—SAM SCALIA

Before our first meeting, Al asked me to send over my new organizational chart for him to review. It was pages! When Al saw all the VPs I had he told me, "If you want me to work with them and not you, this won't work," and he explained why. The next day, I made some big changes!

Al got our organizational chart down to one flat sheet. He also worked with me to redesign our office space. We went from a two-floor "ivory-tower type" design to a one-floor level design with an open floor plan to create visual accountability.

When companies like mine grow fast and big, Al says the tendency is to throw people at the problems versus putting systems and an organizational chart in place that support smart and proper growth. Now we have systems and an organizational chart in place that can get us where we want to go.

—*Sam Scalia, President,*
Samcon Condos, Montreal, Quebec

RECRUITING: OFFERING A CAREER, NOT A JOB

Think of staffing like a constantly moving train where people are jumping on and off at intervals or are getting kicked off—by you! The recruiting process is never-ending because even if you have enough staff, aren't there a couple of staff members you'd love to replace but you don't have the guts to pull the trigger and let them go? Or what if they're really good and they've earned a promotion? Who is on deck to take their spot?

If you wait to recruit, hire, and orient when you're stuck, you'll drop your standards and probably hire out of desperation instead of intelligence.

Good recruiting is equivalent to good marketing. While you need to help customers see the difference between your company and your competition, you also need to demonstrate this difference to potential employees, and that means you have to sell yourself to those prospective employees with a message that *resonates with them.*

Most help-wanted ads are all about what you, the owner, wants. They're about the requirements you demand (most of the time because you're unwilling or incapable of training) or what the company demands (like long hours and low pay . . . only kidding . . . well, maybe not) and very little about what you can offer to the prospective employee that would entice them to learn more about your company or want to join your winning team.

The goal, of course, is to become the employer of choice in the mind of potential applicants.

Take a moment and read over your current want ads. But this time, read them as if you are a job applicant who has a job already but is interested in finding out what else is out there in the job market.

Bet they read differently now.

The bigger question is: What can you offer someone that would entice them to leave their good job and join your company? (After all, the best employees tend to be already employed.)

Is it great wages, a chance for a bonus, health benefits, a 401K, or something more? If you don't have a great list of reasons to join your company, is it because you think you don't have the money to provide all of this?

Great employees make you money, and average or below-average employees—no matter what you pay them—*cost you money.*

I'm not proposing that you overpay your staff, but what I am saying is if your staff is recruited, hired, and oriented the right way, they'll likely be powerfully effective in their role at your company, and finding a way to pay them what they are worth is worth the effort.

Your customers aren't likely to mind spending a few more dollars if in return they get spectacular service from friendly, well-trained staff. It may not be as big a deal as you think. For example, let's say a new toilet is $400. What if you raised the price to $405? If necessary, raise the hourly rate you use to compute your selling price. Two to five dollars (or more) an hour should cover it. (Note: be sure to consult your budget and tweak to make sure it does.)

When it comes to the help-wanted ad, it needs to be written from the perspective of the target person you're seeking to recruit and then run in the types of media that serve your target audience. It also needs to be easy for candidates to respond to your ad!

Like all marketing, it demands a testing period and measurement of the results so you can allocate your advertising dollars accordingly.

Hiring: Efficiency is the Key to Snagging Good Talent

Hiring is typically the interview and testing phase of your candidates. Here's where you try to find out what their strengths and weaknesses are and whether or not they possess willingness. Your ability to hire on willingness versus skills is directly proportional to your ability to provide the skills training they will need. Note: your best employees are typically the ones you build from scratch the right way versus trying to rewire potentially high-skills people with a bad attitude.

When the candidates respond, I believe you should be able to hire them within two weeks, with two good interviews. Too many contractors drag out the process and actually discourage good candidates because they don't enthusiastically welcome the task of recruiting, hiring, and orienting them.

Slots set up for the first interview should cover the following basics:

1. Securing a copy of the interviewee's driver's license if they're going to be driving a company vehicle.
2. Completion of an up-to-date employment application. There are too many rules and regulations to not invest in good help here!
3. A set procedure for questions you'll be asking and what you'll be talking about in general based on the position you're looking to fill.
4. Written testing applicable to the job you're hiring for.
5. Hands-on testing, whether you're hiring a bookkeeper that needs to know QuickBooks or a tech who needs to know plumbing, heating, cooling, or electric.

Here's a tip: when you're interviewing, you will want to get the candidate talking most of the time. It's a lot like a

THE 7-POWER CONTRACTOR | 69

sales call in that you want to ask questions and let them talk so you can write down their responses for future review.

Once you've made the hire, you then need a way to get that person up to speed and immediately feeling like a valuable member of your team. You need an orientation program.

Orienting: All Aboard!

Orientation is where you ensure that employees get off to the best start possible with your company. Your ability to orient them the right way will be directly proportional to the existence and quality of the documented and repeatable systems you have in place (i.e., operations manuals). Optimally, the orientation process should take place over a five-day period. Outline all of the activities by day so that you can make sure not to miss anything.

Here are a few tips for a successful orientation:

1. Have all policies and procedures for the position printed up so you and the new hire can go through them together.

2. Make sure to take the new hire around and introduce them to everyone at your company and help them feel at ease. Then, turn them over to a "big brother" or "big sister" who will show them the ropes.

3. Arrange for ride-alongs for techs and side-by-sides for office staff.

Training: Becoming the Employer of Choice

Offering comprehensive ongoing training can make you the "employer of choice" because it is proof that you are indeed offering prospective employees a career, not just a job.

To make that a reality, however, you must be able to provide all the training employees need to rise up through ranks depicted on your organizational chart and be successful at whatever they're doing at your company, today *and* tomorrow.

The other advantage of formal training is that you can then verify what a new employee knows so they can be entrusted to do the tasks assigned to them. In other words, you don't have to keep mopping up after they've made costly mistakes! We call this getting an employee to "released." It's a lovely place to be, even though it's a never-ending process and the work is never fully done. But the good news is the more you do this process the right way, the better things will go for your customers, your company, and yourself.

Here are some ways my clients teach and verify what a new employee can do:

1. A trainer in the accounts receivable, accounts payable, or credit departments says, "I'll do this task in the manual while you watch and read the manual out loud and let me know if there are any questions," and then does the task.
2. Next the trainer says, "OK, now it's your turn. You sit here and do it and I'll watch you do it."

3. Assuming the trainee performed the task correctly, the trainer then says, "All right, now you enter this invoice, and I'll come back in a few minutes and see how you did."

If the trainee performed the task correctly, and has no questions, the trainer can initial the procedures on a copy of the table of contents of the manual and keep track of progress.

Note: the process is pretty much the same for customer service representatives and dispatchers, but in addition to the reading of the manual there needs to be a lot of phone role plays and recording of calls.

Apprentices should receive your employer-employee manual and a dedicated apprentice manual that directly addresses what they must do in this position and how they can advance their careers within the company. It goes super fast to read through these policies and procedures together. Remember, what you meant when you wrote it in the manual and what employees think it means may be two very different things. Think of all the times you've misinterpreted e-mail communications!

Techs need to have a structured five- to 10-day orientation process. That means besides your stock employer-employee manual they must have a trade manual that addresses the types of tasks your company does and they'll be expected to perform.

If you've committed to building an in-house training center (highly recommended), you can set up problems and expose what the employees do and don't know in a safe environment (read: not at a client's home) and then go about filling in these gaps with training.

Do this and experience for yourself the power of having a company filled with employees who are verified and released!

GROW YOUR OWN TECHS —SAM MARCISSO

Al told me back in the beginning that the best techs you'll ever have are the ones you're going to grow. I understood it, but at first I didn't want to do it because I knew it would take time. I wanted the fix now, so I kept hiring guys off the street. We always thought the next guy who came around the corner was going to be the guy. Well, it never worked. It's rare to find experienced people who will buy into your system and be willing to learn something new.

We finally got tired of it and started hiring kids out of the college program and vocational schools around here. They were young and they were willing and now they are senior techs, and they are producing. The next wave is coming through now and I can see the whole thing coming together. It does take time but we're starting to see the results.

We also do acquisitions and recently we brought on a company that has been around forever. Our culture was totally different than theirs. We inherited some older guys and right out of the gate three of them were gone. They had heard about what we did and they didn't understand it, which is unfortunate. But the ones that trusted us stayed and now they love it. They say stuff like, "Wow, this is great. This is so much better than we had before. We love the systems and people held ac-

countable. You do great and you win extra"—those kind of things. And that feels pretty good.

> —*Sam Marcisso, President,*
> *Pine State Services, Portland, Maine*

CORRECTIVE ACTION

It's never pleasant to discipline someone, let alone fire them, but if they keep screwing up, something has to be done.

It's tempting to avoid these issues altogether and absorb the failures until they explode. The problem is the unwillingness to correct bad behaviors as they occur, in a disciplined and consistent manner, creates unhappy customers and disgruntled staff members, and eats away at an owner's physical and fiscal health.

The good news is when you have written steps for corrective action, and you are willing to enforce them each and every time with each and every person at your company, the process goes better.

I did this at my own company, and my shop steward (this is a top tech who represents the other union staff at the company) came to me one day and said, "We don't fire anybody anymore because of our clear communications, our corrective actions, and our willingness to train. They just choose not to work here anymore!"

Can you believe that?

Where you need to start is with the willingness to discipline someone based on clear written objective measurements, such as a lack of sales for a tech or salesperson based upon a known sales goal, excessive callbacks for a tech that has been verified and released, recordings or observation of customer service representatives who fail to use scripts they are trained on, or a bookkeeper who continues to make mistakes on accounts payable or accounts receivable work.

Corrective action gives employees the opportunity to straighten up. To ensure you are consistent (and lawful) in the way that you do this, you will want to create a corrective action procedure that guides every step.

The corrective action procedure also is something you'll want to include with the employer-employee manual (once it's reviewed by your labor attorney or outside HR vendor).

The corrective action procedure I recommend to my clients has four steps:

- **Step One**: Corrective action begins with a private discussion using written documents such as those in your policy or procedure manuals. Provide the employee with a letter that documents the offense and put a copy of this letter in his or her file. Tell them all is forgiven this time, and let the employee know that if it happens again it will result in a formal write-up.

- **Step Two:** If there is another incident, the next step is a corrective action write-up, which again refers to your written documents. This write-up also can include digital photos or a letter from a customer expressing poor customer service. Let the employee know that if the incident happens again, they will receive a suspension.

- **Step Three:** For a third occurrence, the next step is a suspension of one to two days, with no pay. You also want to present the employee with a document to sign, which acknowledges that they understand the next occurrence will result in immediate termination.
- **Step Four:** If the same thing happens a fourth time, the next step is dismissal. Follow your written guidelines for dismissing an employee. (You'll want to make sure these guidelines also have been reviewed by a labor attorney or outside HR vendor.)

Note: it's important to decide how many corrective actions an employee may have in a quarter so they don't pick a different thing in the manual or in their job to screw up on. You also need to decide which offenses will result in an immediate suspension or dismissal. Examples would be threatening behavior, violation of your drug or alcohol policy, or loss of a driver's license.

Retaining: Nurturing and Growing Your Team

This last step is often the most overlooked. It means you don't neglect the members of your team after they've been onboard for a while.

Instead, you bond with them by finding them doing good work and rewarding them, whether it's with a compliment or compensation. You also must continue to invest in their future by creating a never-ending training process that allows them to steadily grow their careers while simultaneously advancing your business goals.

WALK-AND-TALK MANAGEMENT

One more change in my approach to warding off (if not eliminating) unpleasant five-o'clock visits was to become more proactive in my communications.

I made it a habit to walk around and talk to as many staff members as I could each week, spending a few minutes one-on-one with each of them to ask these three questions:

1. What's going right?
2. What's going wrong?
3. What do I need to know right now?

The fact that I bothered to ask surprised some at first. I practiced actively listening, repeating the essence of what they told me so they knew they'd been heard. Sometimes I took notes as they were talking and made it a point to follow up with them.

And if you adopt this great habit, great things will happen for you and your staff. I say that because of what it did at my own company and what I've seen happen at the com-

THE 7-POWER CONTRACTOR | 77

panies I've worked with. People love to work where they feel they are really listened to.

They won't always get the answer they want, and that's OK. What they are entitled to, however, is one of the following answers, followed by a short explanation if warranted:

1. Yes, we can do that.
2. Yes, we can do that but not right now and here's the reason why.
3. No, we can't do that, and here's the reason why.

Since this three-question method is designed to "take the temperature" of a team member, it should never be a sit-down meeting. It's done as you walk around your office or as you encounter them in the field. The longest any three-question meeting should ever be is five minutes.

I got so good at these impromptu meetings that I could tell pretty quickly who was onboard with us, and who was actively seeking another place to work or would be doing so soon, based on how they responded and whether or not they made eye contact and were smiling!

Just so I'm clear, even with this change in my habits, there was still the occasional surprise. The difference was that in most cases I was able to pick up on what was going on earlier, so I could take action sooner, and that was what reduced my stress.

As you become really proactive, not only will you more easily overcome these bumps in the road, you'll actually be ahead of the curve and well on the way to building a strong and capable team that makes you excited to come to work every day.

Note: A sample organizational chart is included in your Bonus Materials, which you can download using the link and password on the "Bonus Materials" page at the end of this book.

STAFFING POWER: PEARLS

- Don't make employees beg for salary increases; map out a clear career path and performance-based salary levels instead. (Hint: start with an organizational chart.)
- Become the employer of choice by offering a career rather than just a job, complete with thorough ongoing in-house training.
- Make sure your help-wanted ads focus on what's in it for the prospective employee rather than being all about you.
- Once employees are hired, make sure you have a formalized orientation process that will bring them into the fold and set them up for success.
- Sometimes employees screw up. When they do, a written corrective action procedure can help you get the good ones back on track and guide those who don't want to shape up to the door.
- Constantly grow and nurture your existing team by catching them doing good work and rewarding them for it.

Selling Power

I LIVE MOST OF THE TIME in Arizona, which is where I always wanted to be. Eight months out of the year, it's a lovely place to live. The other four months, however, can get just a little toasty. The summer heat puts an awful strain on air conditioners, and a whole lot of other things that my wife and I took for granted back in New York!

Having grown up in the plumbing, heating, and cooling business, I knew that I couldn't push my cooling equipment too long out here without risking a breakdown at the worst time of year. There's only so much a tune-up can do for a 20-year-old heating and cooling system! So I sucked it up and asked three contractors to stop by and take a look at my heating and cooling system, and provide me with a quote. I also made sure to do this well in advance of the height of the cooling season so that neither of us would be stuck doing this work at the busiest time of year.

THREE SELLING SCENARIOS

Since I have been on the other side of selling plumbing and HVAC equipment, I know what it's like and I'm empathetic. So you may be surprised to learn that I actually hate the process of getting prices and meeting contractors. Although I wanted good value, all I was really seeking was a quality job—someone who would engineer the right solution and stand behind their work. And I let each of the three salespeople know this right up front.

I also let them know the former owner, who had custom built the home in the early '90s, had invested in two separate systems, each handling one side of the home. It had always been efficient and I loved that there was a belt *and* suspenders in place, even though I'd never had to use it. If one unit went out, the remaining unit would carry us through. I liked that peace of mind and so wanted to maintain that dual-system configuration. Here's what happened.

THE SHORT CUTTER

Contractor No. 1, recommended to me by a general contractor friend here in Arizona, presented me with a price on the back of his business card after examining the labels on the existing equipment for all of 10 minutes. I asked him if he was going to do a heat loss and heat gain calculation to make sure the new equipment was sized correctly and write out a proposal spelling out what he would provide and do. He informed me that he does this work all the time and so he knows what I need, but I could call in his friend to do the load calculations for about $300. He concluded with a handshake and the statement that his word—and his business card—were his bond.

THE INVISIBLE MAN

Contractor No. 2 was the company that had been servicing our existing equipment for the past 10 years, under two separate service agreements. The salesperson from that company spent a whole hour doing the load calculations and looking the job over in general, which was encouraging.

Two weeks passed without a callback, so I called him. The salesman offered no apology other than to say he was busy. Magically, he was inspired to complete the quote, which he e-mailed to me. The front page of the quote stated that he would have to undersize the air handler on one side of the house because it was the only thing that could fit. Sigh. Fail.

THE PRICEY PROFESSIONAL

Contractor No. 3 was a company my brother had been using to service his vacation home out here. I was actually already familiar with them because one New Year's Day I was at his house checking his heat to make sure it was working, and, sure enough, the heat on one side of the house was out.

I noticed the technicians from this company not only were neatly dressed and courteous, but also dug in and stuck with it until they solved the problem, even though it was a busy holiday.

Later, I saw the owner of this company on our local TV news program. It wasn't a commercial. He was giving good advice on how to ensure you get a proper tune-up on your heating and cooling system—purely educational. Along the way, I learned this guy was an expert with a sterling reputation in the industry.

The salesperson for Contractor No. 3 came by at the appointed time and spent an hour doing the load calculations. Unprompted, he also told me that he saw a problem with the location of one of the existing air handlers, which would restrict the proper sizing of the new units, which were bigger than what I had now. He assured me that he could bring in a contractor and work out how the platform could be lowered to accommodate the properly sized new unit, without any change to the airflow or other issues we discussed.

Contractor No. 3 was selected and they did the work as promised, including stopping back two weeks after the job was done to do a quality inspection.

I asked my wife what she thought of the whole process. She said all she knew was the company we chose always called when they were on their way, wore shoe covers to keep the house clean, and seemed friendly and genuinely interested in making customers for life.

Yes, Contractor No. 3 had made a customer for life. Incidentally, he also was far more expensive than his competitors. My wish for you, of course, is for your company to be more like Contractor No. 3!

BORN TO SELL (NOT)

Improving sales is just like anything else in your business you want to improve. To make quality sales, you need a documented systematic approach, and you need to *practice*.

You also should know that I don't believe there are "born salespeople." That's because I was terrible at first and then I got really good! So good, in fact, that I learned how to teach my salespeople how to make big-ticket sales and how to teach my techs how to sell repairs and appropriate add-on suggestions. None of them were born salespeople either!

They got better because I shared with them the belief that it was in the customer's best interest that we be well prepared and follow a systematic way of selling. This required us to find out what the customer really needed and what they really wanted. We got so good we actually helped customers discover that we had solutions to their nagging problems that they just assumed could not be solved!

CONSISTENCY IS THE KEY

The key to increasing sales is making it possible for many salespeople and many techs to sell in a consistent way.

To do that, you are well served to train your techs and salespeople on how to demystify the sales process for your customer and to build value in all the things your company can do for them. This is what separates you from your competition. Here are some dos and a few don'ts to help you along.

A quick note: some dos and don'ts refer to heating and air conditioning work as examples but we think you'll find the advice is relevant to your contracting service, too.

Do: Ask Good Questions

A great place to start is by asking a good open-ended question that gets the customer talking to you about what is going on today, what they see as a successful outcome, and what they want in the way of comfort, energy savings, and more. You also need to organize the process of what you're going to do when, and what you will show the customer to help them make a good buying decision.

Have two to three questions that technicians habitually ask a customer about their existing comfort and efficiency to make sure they know exactly what the customer desires. This will help them pay special attention to solutions they can offer that are in the customers' best interest.

Note: take notes because the words the customer uses are the ones you want to repeat back as you present them with a solution.

Don't: Skip the Calculations

If the product you are selling requires engineering calculations (a replacement heating and cooling unit, for example), get permission from the customer to do whatever analyses are necessary to make sure you specify the right equipment.

Do: Perform a Visual Survey

If performing a service call, get permission to do a visual survey so you don't miss anything that could be problematic now or in the near future. Making good suggestions on what you can do to take care of any side issues is a good value for everyone because it likely will never become any cheaper to fix than if the customer approves it while you are already there. Note: doing multiple jobs at the time of service deserves a legitimate discount based on knowing your numbers. Also, let the customer know you're going to spend some extra time looking at the trouble spots they have called out to you.

Don't: Condemn Equipment That Is Still OK

If I went to your mom's house and she had a two-year-old water heater, and all I found was that the pilot tube was disconnected and I came upstairs and tried to sell her a brand-new water heater, would you call that ethical selling? How would you feel about me? Not too good. But let me ask you, if I found that the pilot tube was disconnected and I came back upstairs and said, "All I found was the pilot tube disconnected, but while I was there I noticed that the water main valves are really shot, and that's your only emergency shutoff. While I'm here, that's something I can replace. And, I do have one other question: Are you finding that you get all of the hot water you had hoped for when you purchased this two-year-old water heater?" Maybe a whirlpool or hot tub was added or maybe they're just waiting too long for the water to get hot. It's a great opportunity to install a new recirculation line.

Do: Create the Proposal On-Site

As a salesperson, you need to let the customer know how long you will spend on-site creating a customized proposal that you will then go through line by line with them so they know exactly what they will be getting for their hard-earned money. And if you can't do this on-site, you need to let them know when you can come with the proposal and walk through it together.

Don't kid yourself by thinking e-mailing it, faxing it, or mailing it will result in them magically knowing the value of what you selected and how you do that work. It's going to have a negative impact on the amount of closed sales you get.

If you absolutely can't go back, set up a free screen-share program such as Join.me so you can view the proposal and run through it together over the Internet. Even a phone call, where you at least go over the proposal with the customer line by line, will greatly enhance your chances of making the sale.

Don't: Skip Practice Selling

Selling the right way is a skill like all other skills and that means it requires practice. If you have a training center, you're already ahead of the game. If you don't, use your home or your office to simulate tech selling and salesperson selling and watch the money roll in!

Empowering the Process

I was trained on how to do big-ticket sales primarily by my dad, Irving. You ought to know that after all these years I still feel that he was probably the best salesperson I've ever met, and I've met a lot of great salespeople in my life! Also know that I'm not saying he was a great salesperson just because he was my dad.

My yardstick for measuring how good my dad was at big-ticket sales was his close rate. He was a closer. And he closed at a very high rate and for more money than most of his competition. What my dad knew so well was that people buy from people they trust. And people trusted him. I think he radiated trustworthiness because that's how he conducted his life even when nobody was watching.

Dad owed his success to three characteristics:

1. He was persistent but not pushy.
2. He asked good questions and demonstrated that he was really listening.
3. He loved people.

Unfortunately, I didn't inherit his ability through proximity or our shared DNA. At first, I actually tried to copy him, down to emulating his soft voice and mild demeanor. It was a disaster! I eventually realized that if I was to succeed I would have to stop imitating my dad and start being myself.

If you know me, you know I'm passionate and loud. The more excited I get, the louder and faster I talk. Here's the funny thing . . . it worked for me then and it's still working for me today because people sense it's the authentic me talking.

People buy from people they trust. And if you're trying to be someone you're not, they'll sniff it out in a hurry.

My early failure at sales was in many ways actually fortunate because it turned me into a student of sales. It inspired me to pay more attention to what I was doing and to learn—and master—the process of sales.

Buckets of Money—Kathy Betlem

> I wanted to explain how the business worked to my techs, so I borrowed an idea from another contractor who described it using buckets. I said, "See this great big bucket? That's the money we charge and get for doing our job. This smaller bucket, that's the money I use to pay you guys to do the job, the vendors for the material, and the costs of running the office. See this little thimble right here? That's the profit. That's all we get to keep. The more you help us put in there, the more we can share with you."
>
> —Kathy Betlem, Vice President, John Betlem
> Heating and Cooling, Rochester, New York

Yes, Sales Is a Process!

In fact, sales is just as much a process as systematizing how you enter an invoice in your computer or how you make a specific repair for whatever type of contracting trade you're in.

It's also a matter of discipline, starting with what you take from the vehicle in to the sales call and how you go around the home or business looking for a big-ticket sales opportunity.

To be able to follow my dad's example about being persistent and not pushy, I had to get organized. Back in the day, that involved getting an electronic device called a personal digital assistant (PDA). (It was a Palm V for those of you that remember.) The PDA allowed me to set up my phone calls for each day of the week, and see what follow-ups were needed. I never went to bed without addressing each item, either by deleting it because I had closed it, or moving it because it still was in play and needed a follow-up the next day.

Two more tools that allowed me to make a quantum leap in my sales approach were a brag book and a portable file box with hanging folders inside.

CREATING YOUR BRAG BOOK

The brag book was organized to show my customer visual proof that both my company and me were different from my competition in a positive way. I helped them "see it" because I made it visual.

Here's what a good brag book should contain for any successful big-ticket salesperson:

- A picture of someone in your office answering the phones live. The shot of your employee (not a stock photo!) should be of a happy, eager CSR wearing a headset while at their computer. They're sporting a smile because when the customers call, they've been looking forward to serving them.

- Customer testimonials stating how good the company is when it comes to the many types of installation work it did. Testimonials should feature real names, not initials, and if you can get a picture of them, that's even better. Note: one of the most powerful things I learned on my way to becoming a really good salesperson was the power of testimonials. I came to realize that what I said was important to the customer, but what really mattered to them was what other customers they deemed to be like them said about how good my company was or how good I was at helping them through the whole process.

- Before pictures, during-the-job pictures (showing things like how you protected and covered everything), and, finally, a photo of the new install, preferably with the happy customer standing there giving their testimonial about how we were better because we were cleaner, neater, quieter, more respectful, and more responsive. And then having those customers say things like they're now more comfortable, saving money, warmer, cooler, or enjoying their new bathroom or kitchen or remote-controlled heating and cooling system.

Here are some more great things I added to my brag book:

- A picture of a training class working around my training center so I could say, just like my techs were trained to say, "We're not coming to your home today to learn how to do installation work. We're already trained and certified in our in-house training center."
- A picture of all the techs reading from their operations manual (the front of their books showing in the shot) with me leading the class so I could also say, "It pretty much doesn't matter which techs I send to your home since they follow a written checklist procedure for a great installation so we're uniquely able to minimize mistakes and maximize the value of what you purchased."
- A copy of my licensing, certifications, memberships to trade groups, and items like being a member in good standing with the Better Business Bureau.
- Information on how our company drug tests and conducts criminal background checks so they can feel more comfortable about the people who are coming to work at their home or business.
- Finally, I put in all the manufacturers we are certified to use and, in particular, if we are an authorized repair center for a specific line of equipment, I'll make sure to mention this in my presentation.

Are you getting the picture? This worked great because a lot of people are visual and not just auditory. Words are good. Pictures are good. Words and pictures are the best!

I customized this three-ring binder with the multiple company and manufacturer brochures I wanted to show and talk about from the file box that had the multiple hanging folders. And I carried this pre-rigged presentation in a good-looking professional messenger bag. I also had my calculator, laptop, survey questionnaire, blank work orders, and more.

This helped drive me systematically through the sales process, and eventually I didn't have to worry about forgetting any key steps!

Through these structures, sales actually became more natural to me, and more fun, too. I was free to be me and to be effective, and the proof was that I too began closing at a high rate and for a lot more money than the bids I was competing with—just like my dad.

EMPOWERING APPRENTICES—JIM CRINITI

When recruiting and hiring new apprentices, we are always looking for people who are willing and who we think will be comfortable talking to the customer.

To make sure people know whether or not they are cut out for this kind of work, right after orientation all apprentices go to a Sales Power class, where they learn things like how to introduce themselves, where to park the truck, how to get approval for work, and how to overcome price objections and offer suggestions. This happens before we give them any tech-

nical training because so much of their job is really about talking to and serving the customer.

We do this because what causes most callbacks is not a lack of technical skills; it's not being able to talk to the customer to find out what's really going on.

This first class might be called sales training, but in the end it is really about client satisfaction and learning how to correctly diagnose the customer before you try to diagnose their problem.

The Sales Power class also gives us a chance to change apprentices' perception of sales right out of the block. They learn that sales is not about trying to get people to buy things they don't need; it's about getting down to the truth of what's in the customers' best interest, not just today, but in the long term.

Especially now that we do video inspections, there's nothing underground that is a mystery. We are selling solutions that are real and the truth, and that leads to great reviews. Truth and honesty is built right into the process.

Customers want a good price, but they also don't want to have a new problem six months from now or have to take another day off. We also warranty our work, and those warranty calls are our first priority.

They get done before anything else. In most companies, warranty work is last on the list. But we know better. We know that great work results in great reviews and those reviews online will help drive additional sales.

—*Jim Criniti, President, Zoom Drain,*
Philadelphia, Pennsylvania

Full disclosure: Jim Criniti and Jason Criniti, Ellen Rohr,
and I are partner-franchisors for Zoom Franchise Company.
Jim and Jason Criniti are also the owners of the above-
mentioned Zoom Drain franchise, which is located in subur-
ban Philadelphia.

Selling Power: Pearls

- No one is born to sell but all can learn. It is a process and takes practice. So, practice!
- Create an operations manual for selling that calls out how you sell so that everyone is selling consistently across your company.
- Create selling tools that contain both pictures and words. Some people are visual learners.
- Be persistent, but not pushy. Ask good questions.
- Most important, be yourself. Authenticity builds trust and trust means customers for life.

[|]

Marketing Power

YEARS AGO, I was knocking back a beer at a Super Bowl party when I overheard a conversation that shocked me.

"My company's the best, and you're an idiot if you don't agree," boasted one of the guests.

"How would you know who's got the best heating company?" the other asked. "You wouldn't be able to find your boiler if your life depended on it!"

I found this conversation fascinating. I'd never heard two people argue over who had the better heating company!

At the time, I was still working in my family's plumbing, heating, and cooling business on Long Island, so I said, "I'm in the heating business. What companies do you guys use?"

They said different names, and both were my companies. Neither had a clue that the other guy's company was actually the same one!

That's because at the time, my dad, my brothers, and I believed that as we acquired new heating companies the

customers would feel more comfortable if the name re-
mained the same. So we kept the familiar name on the
trucks and the invoices. This experience made me realize
what a blunder this was.

When I got to the office the next day, I told my dad and
brothers what had happened at the Super Bowl party. They
couldn't believe that people were confused by our names. I
told them to try to see it through the customers' eyes, and
you could see the lightbulbs go on.

We needed to come up with one name and one image.

My dad immediately reached for the phone.

"Who are you calling?" I asked.

"Just an old friend who owns an advertising agency in
New York City," he said.

TRUSTING LEO

Up until then, our only advertising had been a small yellow
pages ad and the occasional modest ad in the local paper,
which we let the people at the paper write. They would ask
for a few ideas about what we were selling, and that was
that.

Dad's friend, Leo, worked for larger clients than us, but
because they were childhood friends, Leo agreed to help. He
asked that my dad assign one of us to him for the duration
of the campaign and Dad chose me.

Leo wasted no time in establishing the ground rules for
our working relationship:

- **Rule One**: I'd need to study what my competition did
  well and tell Leo why I thought it was working.

- **Rule Two**: I'd need to understand what was unique about us and why it mattered to our customers.
- **Rule Three**: I'd need to trust Leo, especially when he wanted to do something new and bold.

"So, what made your dad call me after all these years?" Leo asked.

I told him about the conversation between the guys at the Super Bowl party. I emphasized that our goal was to clarify that we were one company. "And . . ." I hesitated, a little ashamed to finish my thought.

"Yes, and what else?" Leo said.

"My second goal is to convince all those people who don't use us now to start!"

Leo laughed. "Why would you bother to advertise if you weren't interested in selling to everyone?" he said. "You need to say something specific to someone or you risk saying nothing to everyone. Al, do you know the difference between marketing and advertising?"

"Aren't they the same thing?" I said.

"No," he said. "Advertising is a vital part of marketing, but just a part. Newspaper, radio, television, billboard, and yellow page ads are different forms of advertising." (Note: that's all we had back then, but now we've also got websites, AdWords, mobile apps, and more.)

He continued: "Marketing includes all of these and more. A big element of marketing is projecting a uniform image to everyone who comes in contact with your company. This determines the way you answer your phones, the way your trucks look to the public, how your staff dresses, and even more. Are you beginning to see the difference?"

I was.

"Good, because we're not just going to advertise your new name and image, we're going to *market* it. That means you have to be determined to get the entire company to project the image that we'll be marketing. And the toughest part will be to keep it up."

At our second meeting, Leo unveiled his plan:

- He'd tailor our message to the advertising vehicle we would be using. For example, he explained that an effective billboard should be very visual and contain no more than five words.

- He'd create an image and message that we would repeat in all that we did. He told me that when I got sick of the message, it would be just starting to sink in to the minds of our audience.

- He wouldn't write boring copy. But he wouldn't get so clever that the message got lost.

- He'd advertise intensively over a short period because that was better than advertising too little over a longer period.

Leo and I discussed the budget, which would determine the choices he could make on where to place ads, and how frequently. He settled on bus billboards, billboards at the railroad station, billboards on major local roads, a large newspaper that served our marketing area, a news talk radio station, and ads on the back of milk cartons. (Today Leo likely would have included a regularly updated blog, a search engine optimized website, and social media channels such as Facebook, Instagram, and Twitter.)

Since this was going to be, by far, our biggest marketing effort to date, we also allocated money to repaint our trucks, supply uniforms for our technicians and logo shirts for the salespeople, and print new letterhead, envelopes, and stationery. We would train our staff on how to answer the phone with our new name and create a specific on-hold message for each season.

Leo wrote a letter that we sent to our existing customers. He used a conversational tone. It explained how we were just changing the name, not the service they had come to love.

"Why are we using so many different ways of advertising?" I asked.

"The first time people see your name it doesn't register, but it does go into their subconscious. And the more they see or hear your name, the more they'll remember it." I nodded.

"Do you know the two reasons a company should change its name?" he asked. I shook my head. "Either to announce that companies are merging, or to distance itself from trouble. Luckily for you, you're just getting all your companies married. The name should be something the customers already know, something the companies have in common."

The problem was we were using five different names for our companies! And we wondered why people were confused! Leo wrote them down and played around with different choices. He settled on Oil Services Inc. (OSI, for short) and created a logo for us.

"Now, let's select a unifying new color for your trucks," he said.

"The law in NYC requires that fuel oil trucks be green," I said. "And not just any color green. Only one of these six will do."

"OK," he said, pointing at one of the six shades. "This will do nicely."

"But that's the ugliest green on the page. It sticks out like a sore thumb," I said.

"Which is precisely why I picked it," he said.

"But . . ."

"Al, when you have doubt, remember Rule No. 3: Trust Leo. I'm not asking you to wear a suit this color. I want your trucks to be visible at a distance and this will do the trick. And when you paint the new OSI logo on your trucks, put it near the back of the truck, not in the center. And tilt it at a 45-degree angle. And you know how your current trucks have phone numbers, radio towers, and boiler installation promotions? From now on, the only thing I want to see on your trucks is your new name and logo. If they're interested, they'll find your name in the phone book and call." (Today, of course, they would just Google it!)

We used to cram a lot of information on our trucks. We figured we were paying for the whole space so we covered every inch. We listed every phone number (we had four), we showed the areas we serviced, we mentioned that we had 24-hour service, and we had a painted radio tower to prove that we were radio dispatched. We also had signs letting people know we installed boilers, water heaters, and on and on.

I visualized this bright green truck with the off-center logo and I figured the staff would think I had lost my mind.

But I did trust Leo.

Once we had the trucks painted, it suddenly looked like we had twice as many trucks on the road. While driving around town, people would see the distinctive green of our trucks with the new logo from blocks away. We were different!

Even my competitors called. They said they liked the new look!

Now the only name our customers saw was OSI. And OSI became everybody's favorite heating company at most Super Bowl parties from then on.

You'll note that even though this example is more than two decades old, the marketing principles Leo followed still hold true. The marketing tools and channels have evolved over time, but the principles of good marketing never change.

Marketing is one of two responsibilities that permanently belong to the owner (the other is financial). The responsibility for the image and associations you need to create in the minds of your customers are too important to transfer to someone else.

You can delegate, but you must never abdicate your responsibility for marketing—or, like the two Super Bowl guys, your customers may not see your company the way you want and need them to see it.

BACK TO BASICS—JIM CRINITI

Before learning about Marketing Power, we were doing what a lot of companies do, which was to shout at the market as much as possible in hopes that people would hear and call us. It was a buckshot approach. We didn't have a plan or a budget. If someone offered us a chance to put our name on shopping carts, or sponsor a local youth baseball team, or buy an ad in a church bulletin, we did that. We were kind of bebopping around trying different things, and not a lot was happening.

Al had us put together a marketing manual that called out the customers we were going after and the detailed marketing allocation, budget, and calendar. Right away things seemed less chaotic because the manual outlined all of our decisions: "Here's the amount of sales we're going to allocate toward marketing, here's what we're going to do and when we're going to do it, and here's how we're going to measure the results." We just had to follow what it said.

The funny thing is that the Marketing Power process actually led us back to what we were doing to build the business at the very beginning, which was to contact people directly and ask them for business until they either gave it to us or told us to go away!

For example, as drain- and sewer-cleaning specialists, at first a lot of our work came from other plumbing contractors. We made a list of the top 25 plumbing contractors in the area and set a goal to get all their work, and, one by one, we did. We mailed them postcards, called them, made site visits, and called again, nonstop. And it worked.

At some point we stopped doing it, probably because it is a lot of work. I think we thought maybe there was some secret sauce out there that would make it easier, or a commercial, postcard mailing, or yellow pages ad that would make customers come running, but we found out there's no magic pill. You have to do the work.

Through Marketing Power, we were able to look at all of our options and see that we needed to get back to referral marketing and using our testimonials. The marketing manual is great because it brings you back to the center, and keeps you from coloring too far outside the lines.

One thing we put in place recently was the marketing calendar. Zoom is pretty busy in the winter, so it seems like that would be the last time you'd want to do marketing, but there is stuff you need to do so that when April rolls around there is still business coming in the door. The only way to make sure the right calls are coming in, at the right time, from the right customers, is to plot it all out on a calendar and then follow your plan.

As Al says, that's how you step off a curb during slow times rather than falling off a cliff.

In terms of allocation, at first we were heavy on yellow page ads. Now we focus the bulk of our budget on SEO and the rest is divided between referral marketing and socking away some money for acquisitions. We don't do anything with yellow pages any more.

The best part is that the Zoom Drain Long Island franchisee has adopted our online marketing strategy and they are seeing a 5:1 return on their investment right now.

—*Jim Criniti, President, Zoom Drain,*
Philadelphia, Pennsylvania

THE THREE RIGHTS AND THREE MUSTS OF MARKETING

Leo helped us create a unified image for our company, making it easier for us to make our audience aware of our presence in the community. But cleaning up and unifying an image is actually just one component of a larger marketing *system*. Like other systems, a marketing system is composed of numerous critical components.

THE THREE MARKETING RIGHTS

If a marketing system is built properly, all the different components in it work together to create three specific "right" conditions:

1. The right amount of calls
2. From the right customers
3. At the right time

Why is this so important? Because generating too many calls from difficult or bargain-hunting customers can actually end up hurting your business—especially if you are already jammed with work or don't have enough properly trained techs to do the work you've already sold!

To achieve these optimal conditions, you need to determine these three things:

1. What type of customers you really want
2. When they will likely want your services
3. What bandwidth you have available to serve them

Once you know these things, you can decide what kind of marketing you need to do, when you need to do it, and what you need to spend on it to get the phone to ring with the right number of great customers at the right time.

The decisions about what type of marketing activities you will do are typically recorded in a document called a marketing plan.

THE THREE MARKETING MUSTS

To be effective, a marketing plan must contain the following three elements:

1. Marketing Budget: How much money you have to spend on marketing over the next 12 months
2. Marketing Allocation: A list of exactly what you're going to spend that money on
3. Marketing Calendar: A 12-month calendar that denotes exactly when each marketing effort will take place and for how long

When determining your marketing budget you'll want to base that number on an objective benchmark, such as percentage of sales, rather than the subjective and patently dangerous "what (we think) we can afford."

Without a consistent and significant investment in marketing, you risk losing more business than you replace. Using a percentage of sales ensures that as your business grows so do the resources invested in marketing it. The most conservative number I ever recommend is four percent of sales and most of the time it's more like 10 percent. For my bigger clients that number often increases to 15 to 20 percent of sales, because they are skilled marketers who know what efforts will produce the results they're looking for.

However, if you're like most of my clients, the marketing calendar is the "must" that will mess you up the most. The time most people remember their marketing calendar is when the phone stops ringing—and by then it's too late. Now you've got to try to crank up the marketing machine to drum up business fast and avoid the cliff.

See if any of this sounds familiar:

"Did anyone call the radio station and set up those ads?" No.

"Did we ever get that quote from the printer on those doorknob hangers?" No.

"Did we ever get a list from the direct-mail people?" No.

You get the picture.

To make a marketing system work, you, the owner, must live by your marketing calendar so you can ensure that marketing activities are taking place consistently throughout the year. That way when the slow times come—as they always do—instead of at the precipice, you will already be in motion, ahead of the game, and, with any luck, ahead of your competitor as well.

FIVE WAYS TO MARKET AT LOW OR NO COST

I realize you could be thinking, "Marketing is a whole lot easier if you've got a lot of money to spend," and you would be correct.

But marketing is also a great way to go broke if you don't have a plan and don't know what you're doing.

This was as true back in the good old days when you could take out a double-truck ad in the yellow pages and either get really rich or really poor, depending on how many books you needed to be in and how many competitors were also trying to get to the front of those categories in the same books.

Today, the goal is the same but the channels have changed. Now it's about making it to the top of the list on Google or at least the first page of the search results, through search engine optimization (SEO).

There are tons of ways to improve your SEO ranking by spending money on things like pay per click (PPC). This too is a way to get really rich or really poor if you don't know what you're doing or hire the wrong people to manage it. (For example, your business is based in Phoenix but you or your vendor doesn't have it set up to repel people clicking through to other areas that you don't service, like Philadelphia.) If you're going to hire someone to help with SEO, make sure you talk to former clients and verify their results.

If you currently have both the problem of not enough calls and not enough money to spend on SEO or other more expensive marketing tactics, there are many low- and no-cost marketing tactics that won't break the bank. Here are just a few.

YARD SIGNS AND CLOVERLEAFING

Yard signs are a way to get your name out in front of the neighbors of the customer you're working for. People like to hire the plumbing, heating, cooling, or other company that's already serving their immediate neighborhood.

When you use yard signs, I recommend you set a goal for the company about how many yard signs you want to get out there every month (and every year) and engage your whole team in making it happen.

Cloverleafing is leaving doorknob hangers at the nearby homes of the customer you have just provided service to. This should be done year-round but at the very least during your slow season. It helps to increase your customer base by referencing satisfied customers in their neighborhood who already used your services and can testify to the benefits of doing so.

The best way to get this done on a call is to have an apprentice (if you have an apprentice program) or the tech hit the four to six neighbors on either side that are not already your customers. (Make sure to check your database!) Be sure to spot-check to verify compliance.

PUBLIC AND MEDIA RELATIONS

Public and media relations involves consistently reaching out to the local media with useful information that will interest their readership if they're a newspaper, listeners if they're a radio station, and viewers if they're a TV station. The goal is to establish yourself as their go-to person for information, tips, and advice related to whatever trades you do. Sending out well-written press releases and finding ways to meet journalists in person—at networking events, for example—are just a few ways to let the media know you're out there as their expert.

In addition to providing free exposure, media coverage can also be listed on your website, where it becomes implied third-party endorsements of what makes you different from your many competitors in a way that money can't buy.

POSTCARDS

Correction: Laser-focused testimonial-based direct-mail postcards. This postcard type features a photo of an actual happy customer, captioned with their full name and the town in which they live. Potential customers will be much more apt to trust your message if it's accompanied by a real person, who they perceive is just like them, endorsing it.

You can order and purchase mailing lists with the names and addresses for these "ideal" customers from providers such as www.infousa.com or www.coleneighborhoods.com.

These direct-mail pieces need to be assembled and ready to go when you think things *will be* slowing down. Waiting until there's little or no work to mount a campaign is too late. Also, you're wasting your money, in my opinion, if you don't mail the piece out three times over a six-week period so there are enough touches to judge the effectiveness of the campaign.

REFERRAL MARKETING

Referral marketing is one of the most powerful marketing strategies. One satisfied customer who is willing to recommend you to their friends, relatives, and acquaintances is what you're after here. There should be some reward for them doing this. It can be a discount coupon for both the new customer and the person who referred you, or even a reward program. You also want to encourage them to brag about you and post pictures of their neatly installed furnace on social media.

Also consider tapping into fellow contractors who provide services to your target market but don't directly compete with you. An example would be creating an active referral marketing arrangement with a company that specializes in home alarm systems. That's great if you do plumbing, heating, and cooling only. But make sure you know the contractor and their reputation, because if they mess up at your customers' homes and you recommended them, your reputation will be tarnished with the same brush.

SOCIAL MEDIA

Social media is making use of outlets like Facebook, Twitter, Instagram, and LinkedIn to establish and maintain a connection with prospective customers where they already hang out. The key to success here is to make sure you are ready to put out a steady stream of interesting and *appropriate* content that your prospects will be interested in.

Be aware that really strong social media shouldn't be totally delegated. Even if you have professional help with supplying content and distribution, you want to make sure that what is going out is in your voice so it can reinforce the uniqueness of you and your company. You also want to make sure nothing accidentally goes out over social media that could potentially reflect poorly on your company. (It happens more often than you think.)

Again, there's a whole lot you can do on your own here that will go a long way toward making low-cost and no-cost marketing pay off. And, done strategically with key vendors, you can further multiply the return on a modest investment.

Note: A marketing allocation spreadsheet and sample calendar is included in your Bonus Materials. Download them using the link and password on the "Bonus Materials" page at the end of this book.

MARKETING POWER: PEARLS

- Advertising is just one element of marketing.
- Marketing is also about creating and demonstrating a professional image to your marketplace.
- The goal of marketing is to get the right number of calls from the right customers at the right time.

- The three marketing musts are budget, allocation, and calendar. Together, they make up your marketing plan.

- Yard signs and cloverleafing, public and media relations, direct-mail postcards with testimonials, referral marketing, and social media are examples of low- or no-cost marketing.

Sales Coaching Power

DON'T YOU JUST HATE having to give annual holiday bonuses that are more out of obligation than something the employee deserves? It's not that owners are Scrooge; it's just that to give annual holiday bonuses too many of us end up having to take money out of our own bank accounts or, worse, from our own holiday funds!

Also, once you give a certain size bonus to a staff member based on something that's not objective, it's pretty near impossible to take it away or even lower it, and that stinks.

It's time to stop this merry-go-round and create a bonus program that makes sense and rewards the right stuff.

REWARD THE RIGHT STUFF

There are two main ways to reward the right stuff. One is called the company-wide bonus game, and the other is a series of goals and spiffs that comprise an overarching bonus and compensation program. The goal of both of these programs is to provide bonuses with money that your employees create.

As its name implies, the company-wide bonus game is for everyone on staff, while the bonus and compensation program is designed to reward employees who perform work directly for the customer (i.e., service technicians, installers, and big-ticket salespeople).

THE COMPANY-WIDE BONUS GAME

Implementing this program takes some planning and preparation, so if you want to be ready to go by the next holiday season, I recommend you begin as soon as you are ready.

By ready, I mean you are at a known financial position (KFP) and you are operating with a current budget. If you are not yet at a KFP, and you aren't yet operating from a budget, do that first. To be able to track and make sure this system is working properly, you need those two things to be in place.

It's worth repeating: do not implement this or any other type of self-funded bonus program until you are at a KFP! (Once you are at a KFP, however, get it going right away!)

Here's how this self-funded bonus program works. Through the budgeting process, you will have determined your annual salary expenses and operational expenses, and the profit you wish to make to arrive at an annual sales goal.

Typically, a bonus program is equal to two to three percent of annual salary. (Commissions don't count because you can't know that number when you do the budget.) That two to three percent number (whatever you decide) is then *added* to your annual sales goal in the budget (which is why you can't wait until it's the holiday season to begin).

If employees hit that annual sales and profitability target, they get the bonus, and we are happy to pay it.

Since everyone on staff participates in this game, everyone needs to understand how it is played. Since bonuses are now self-funded, employees are only rewarded based upon hitting the goals, which means they actually pay themselves the bonus!

One of the best things about the company-wide bonus game is that it takes you out of the role of having to "motivate" your staff. They will understand the benefits of playing the game you describe, especially if you post the statistics in a public place, for all to see, and talk up the results.

The company-wide bonus game can also help your company come together by helping staff members understand the impact—and interdependence—of the different roles. That how the customer service representative handles the call, the dispatcher maximizes production, and the tech handles the service call affects not just the company sales and profitability goals but also what ultimately goes into their own pockets!

Bonus and Compensation Program

The bonus and compensation program is designed to reward employees who perform work directly for the customer. Those who get to play here are your service techs, your big-ticket salespeople, and your installers.

The best way to inspire action is to create some competition within the ranks, such as:

- A weekly and monthly bonus game for service techs that sell additional service work based on *individual sales goals*. (The company's sales goal is what it costs to operate. You'll also want to be sure that your managers' personal sales goals and bonuses are aligned with both the techs' goals and the company's goals.)
- Weekly and monthly spiffs for installers who are able to bring the job in on time or ahead of schedule with no callbacks for 30 days.
- Weekly and monthly bonus games for salespeople for best closing rate and total sales. I recommend basing the calculations on projected labor and materials versus actual labor and materials with the desired gross profit achieved. Doing it this way removes the reward for underbidding a job just to make a sales number.

You'll need some written rules of engagement and a commitment to tracking and reporting progress of course, but between these two approaches you should be able to reward your employees for a job well done with the money they were instrumental in bringing in.

REWARDING THE RIGHT STUFF—JIM CRINITI

We used to hate giving out bonus checks because of how our bonus program was designed; in fact, we used to get kind of mad when people made sales, which, when you think about it, is a little crazy. One time we decided to give away a 50-inch TV. But no one was even trying for it. As it turned out, everyone already had a TV that was bigger!

We tried a lot of other gimmicks, like a spinning wheel for a prize based on sales, but they all created the same problem. We still had to pay out and that meant less profit for us.

Now we reward people based on customer service, labor as a percentage of sales, close rate, and other factors that make us feel good about what they are producing. So when we write that check, we can feel good about it because the bonus comes out of sales they created that were above and beyond what we originally planned for in the budget.

Our techs post their sales on a whiteboard in the training room every week. If they make their goal, they get to write that number in green. If they don't, they have to write it in red. Techs do not want to come up to that board and have to write in red. It hurts them. It's not just about the money; it's that they want to do well and feel proud that they wrote their number in green.

We have one technician who really hustles. He makes a 20 percent bonus every month. He used some of it to buy furniture and now he's saving for a house. It's nice to know a young kid like that can hustle and then take that money and save for his future. It's a great system because everybody wins.

—Jim Criniti, President, Zoom Drain,
Philadelphia, Pennsylvania

SALES COACHING 1-2-3

Assuming your tech, installer, and sales staff have received adequate (and preferably ongoing) sales training, they should already understand what's expected of them in the field, and be familiar with the procedure for identifying and offering to the customer additional services and products that would genuinely add to their comfort and safety. The spirit of the game is first and foremost to provide the best service possible to your customers. Sales bonuses are for good sales, sales that sit well with customers because you deliver what is needed and wanted.

To effectively manage the staff involved you'll need to provide sales coaching on three tiers—meeting, exceeding, and missing company expectations. It looks like this:

1. You've reached your sales goal? Great. We love you, you keep coming to work, but there is no bonus.
2. You've gone $1 above your goal. Excellent. We'll generously share part of it with you in a bonus.
3. You've missed your goal by $1. OK. We will coach you for a period of time. If after coaching you still can't make it, we'll have you go help some other company.

Optimally, there would always be training available for staff members who want to get better at the sales craft and make even more money for both of you!

Don't Expect What You're Unwilling to Inspect

If you stay in the office because you believe that your techs, installers, and salespeople are always doing things the right way and being ethical, you're headed for trouble. To minimize chances of trouble and bad things happening as a result, you must be willing to check up on people.

To make sure you have a handle on what is actually going on in the field, mystery shopping and ride-alongs are *essential*. And as you put the new rewards programs in place, these tools will become even more important.

Mystery shopping and ride-alongs aren't meant to be punitive, but rather to catch people doing something right so you can make a big deal of it. That said, you also want to be the one to catch something unethical or dangerous before your company ends up on the evening news and is driven out of business!

Sales coaching, bonus programs, and measurement and verification processes that are designed in this way are a win-win-win for customers, staff, and owners alike.

RIDE-ALONGS—JASON CRINITI

We realize that technicians are people, not robots, so if we see someone is struggling we don't just leave them out there, we get in the truck with them and ride along to find out what's going on and how we can help. The results of doing this can be pretty awesome.

We have a field supervisor here named Steve who is rising through the ranks. He was one of the first to graduate from our apprentice-to-technician program, where we fully train new hires from scratch in our own training center. Steve had been out on the road for a month or two and was doing fine technical work, but when it came to sales, things weren't going so well. To be able to help, I needed to see what was happening, so I decided to join him in his truck for a ride-along.

Steve closed small additional sales on our first and second calls, but call three was a different story. Steve offered some additional options to the customer as he had been trained to do. The customer objected and became defensive, saying, "I had no idea it would be so expensive. I wasn't expecting that!"

Steve looked down and then over to me.

I realized he didn't know what to do or say to overcome their price objection! I stepped in and began educating the customer and we managed to salvage the job.

Back in the truck, I asked Steve, "So what do you think you did wrong?"

He said, "Well, I only closed two jobs."

I said, "Yes, but those two were emergencies where the customer really didn't have a choice. The other one didn't close because the customers had price objections. When that happens, the first thing you need to do is ask this one question: 'Why do you think it's too high?' Just get the customer to answer that question and then you can start to educate them."
We went back over the problem calls and role played to make Steve more comfortable with asking the simple question.

Optimally, I would have done another ride-along with Steve the next day, but as it turned out, it was a few weeks before I had time to do another. The day of the second ride-along, after diagnosing the problem, we met up with a customer who was accompanied by his next-door neighbor, and we already could tell it was going to be a problem.

I leaned over and said to Steve, "Just remember what we talked about."

Steve presented the solution to the customer, and he complained, "That's an awful lot of money! How am I going to pay $800 to clear drains?"

Then the neighbor, a know-it-all, chimed in. "I used a guy; he was cheap. I could call him up," he said.

Oh boy, here we go, I thought.

But instead of looking down at his shoes, this time Steve turned to the neighbor and began to educate him on our service. When the neighbor realized Steve was holding his ground, he excused himself and went back to his house.

Next, Steve asked the customer, "So what do you think about the job?" He had successfully fended off the know-it-all neighbor, and he got the job.

From that day on, Steve's confidence level soared and he closed more sales than ever.

I know he felt good, but as his coach and manager, I felt good too.

I've learned that less is more. Sometimes one or two simple suggestions is all a tech needs to turn the situation around. But without being in the truck to see what actually is happening out in the field, it's hard to know where the problem is or what they really need to hear. If you want to get to the bottom of a problem in the field, ride-alongs are the way to go.

—Jason Criniti, Service Manager, Zoom Drain,
Philadelphia, Pennsylvania

SALES COACHING POWER: PEARLS

- Reward employees with money they create.
- Don't undertake a self-funded bonus program without being at a known financial position and having a budget.
- Provide sales coaching on three tiers—meeting expectations, exceeding expectations, and missing expectations.
- Trust but verify what is going on out in the field through mystery shopping and ride-alongs.

Bonus: Leadership Power

MAYBE YOU'RE WONDERING why we didn't start with leadership. After all, you are the *leader* of your company.

The answer is that it makes little sense to try teaching you how to build a bigger, better business boat when the one you are on is in the process of sinking! Now that you know what to do to fix the boat, we can talk about the seven powers and leadership.

The seven powers are designed to help you build a bigger and better boat, one that is able to get you where you want to go faster. And *where you want to go* ultimately is what Leadership Power is all about.

Leadership Power is where you want to go; Planning Power is what you'll do, when you'll do it, and how you'll get there.

That's right, Planning Power involves leadership, too. Someone has to decide which five projects your company is working on! In fact, the two are permanently linked.

Leadership is one thing. Leadership *Power* is becoming way more conscious of what you are working on, based on where you ultimately want to end up, and then creating and executing a plan that will make it so.

THE 10 GOLDEN RULES

What most people don't realize is that to achieve this, all of your goals—*personal and business*—must be in sync.

For example, I once had a consulting call with a contractor who said that he was currently at $1 million in sales and wanted to increase sales to $25 million in three to five years. But when I inquired about his personal goals, he said one of them was that he really wanted to be able to achieve this goal while sitting on a beach and not doing any work.

Knowing what I know about what it would actually take to achieve that kind of growth, I can tell you those personal and professional goals are not in sync!

One way you can ensure your goals are in sync is to create a list of 10 golden rules for running your business and 10 golden rules for running your life, and then work them back and forth until they are in sync.

It's probably easier to show rather than tell you exactly what I mean by these rules, so take a look at mine.

10 GOLDEN RULES FOR AL LEVI'S BUSINESS

1. The business functions seamlessly whether I am in Phoenix, New York, or on the road.
2. The business is fun and challenging.

3. The business helps improve the quality of the lives of both the owners and employees I work with.

4. The work I do becomes an integral part of the company and I am responsive to clients but it doesn't require I take a phone call at 3 a.m.

5. The business is able to turn a profit and provide benefits, such as vacations and health insurance.

6. The business has real products to sell to clients, products that will work for them whether I am there or not.

7. The business allows me to teach what I've learned and to learn what I want to know so that I'll be able to teach others.

8. The business becomes known as the "expert" in what we do.

9. The business is able to "fire" a bad client.

10. The business allows for free time to play golf two to three times a week, exercise three times a week, study, travel, and be available for my family.

10 Golden Rules for Al Levi's Life

1. Live in Phoenix eight months a year and New York during the summer.

2. Do stimulating work and hobbies.

3. Take nice vacations.

4. Keep learning.

5. Keep teaching.

6. Take pride in whatever I do by pursuing a path to master the subject.

7. Associate with positive people.
8. Play golf two to three times a week.
9. Exercise three times a week for 30 minutes.
10. Be available for my family.

Do you see how one set of rules syncs with and supports the other? What are your golden rules?

START WITH YOUR END GAME

Once you know what you want to create, you are ready to start thinking about your end game. End game options range from staying in the business until *The End*, to closing your doors completely, and a number of options in between.

The first step, however, is to make an honest and objective assessment of your business on four levels:

1. What your business is worth today to someone interested in buying it
2. What's working and will continue to work
3. What's not working and why
4. What you want your business to do for you versus what you have to do for it

Next, you need to take an objective look at both your personal assets and the business assets and assess what you will need to live the lifestyle you desire. Professional help from a certified financial planner (CFP) can be a big help here.

Then, it's time to get real.

Most of us forget that we went into business for a reason. Those reasons vary but typically it's the desire for financial freedom, a chance to be our own boss, to build a legacy that we can pass on to our family, and our desire to enjoy success.

Unfortunately, we get so busy with dealing with the day to day of business that it can become so overwhelming that we don't take the time to look ahead and plan.

I get it.

That said, I encourage you to think of this approach to running your business as if you were driving your car with your eyes on the road ahead versus driving your car while texting. You're going to crash at some point. It's just a matter of when.

SHAPING END-GAME STRATEGY

When shaping your end-game strategy you have the following six options:

1. Fix what's wrong with your business, fall in love with the work you do, and regain your health.

2. Take on a partner to help shoulder the load. Just make sure there's due diligence about who you're getting "married to" and make sure exits are in place just in case the honeymoon ends!

3. Create a transition plan that allows younger family members or management to take the helm as you

begin to step out. This also takes planning, including exits for all.

4. Sell the business to an outsider and go do something else—business, pleasure, or volunteering.

5. Sell the business to your employees. How cool is it when those who have worked for you can begin to work for themselves as you head toward your next phase in life? Note: only do this if your business is systematic and there is a management team in place that you know can run it; otherwise, you risk getting dragged back in.

6. Close the doors. This can be the most positive option if the business can't be sold and you know that every day you stay in business you're digging a deeper hole. There is no shame in doing this if you're not committed to the longer and tougher road of fixing the broken business. The only shame is in continuing to spin your wheels if you're not willing to do what it takes to get out of the ditch!

The biggest thing is to plan, gain clarity, get help in this process if you need it, and then *act*. Procrastination will rob you of your options. And that's no way for the game to end.

LEADING OTHERS

If the course you've charted includes building a thriving business, great! Then you will need to communicate that vision in a way that inspires others to assist you in getting where you want to go.

Remember back in Planning Power where we talked about the concept of working on the right things, at the right time, in the right way? And the template for rolling out the top five projects on a whiteboard with enthusiasm?

That's leadership.

MANAGEMENT VERSUS LEADERSHIP

If you're an owner who started as a technician, as most of us have, you could be accidentally mashing up leadership and management when they are very different roles. One way to describe it is, "A leader steers the ship away from the iceberg; a manager is busy arranging the deck chairs." Another is, "Management is deciding where to put the ladder; leadership is deciding what wall you want it to lean against."

There is a time to be both a leader and a manager, but leadership always comes first.

ON THE SAME PAGE—KATHY BETLEM

Our business planning process used to sound like this: "Now we're at five million; how about eight?" "OK." No clue how to get there. Let's just jump off the bridge and hope at the bottom there's eight million dollars. How would you know? There's a difference between tossing a number out there and actually getting there by calculating it.

Now our conversation sounds like, "OK, we need three trucks. If we had three trucks, we could do this, and that would get us to here revenue wise." Once we have that goal, then we can figure out what projects or habits we need to work on to get there.

When my brothers and I were working on our three-year plan recently, we wrote down our own goals first. When we compared notes, all three of us had added the same number of technicians and the same amount of revenue! We were all on the same wavelength. As the numbers person, I figured I would have it figured out, but I didn't know that they would! But we've learned so much from Al and Ellen that we are now able to look into the future and see where we can be. It's very cool!

—Kathy Betlem, Vice President, John Betlem
Heating and Cooling, Rochester, New York

LEADERSHIP POWER: PEARLS

- Business and personal goals must be in sync. What are your 10 golden rules for each?
- Starting with your end game in mind increases the chances that your plan actually will get you where you want to go.
- Know the six options: fix, partner, transition, sell to outsider, sell to employees, or close. All are equally valid depending on the situation.
- Management is deciding where to put the ladder; leadership is deciding what wall you want it to lean against.

The Road to Success

AS A KID, I remember the whole family watching the movie *The Wizard of Oz* whenever it was on TV. Oz was pretty cool even when I watched it with my brothers and sisters in black and white. Imagine how cool it was when we actually saw it for the first time in color!

Beyond the movie, I was mesmerized by the story of good and evil and the journey to the promised land of Oz. The first time I saw it, as a little kid, I was terribly frightened by the Wicked Witch and her flying monkeys. And when Dorothy, Tin Man, Scarecrow, and Lion first met the Wizard of Oz, his foreboding giant face and booming voice was also all too scary.

Just as in life, what's scary at first can become a lot less scary when we peel away the facade or, in this case, look behind the curtain and see for ourselves that the Great and Terrible Wizard of Oz was nothing more than an ordinary man who used a big screen projector and a voice amplifier.

What the Wizard of Oz did have, however, was the great power of insight. He could see in others what they were not able to see in themselves.

You'll remember that the movie ends with the now-exposed Wizard of Oz helping Tin Man, Scarecrow, Lion, and Dorothy see that what they were seeking from him was something they had inside all along. All they needed was a mentor to help them look inside and believe in themselves.

HEART, BRAINS, AND COURAGE

I'm no wizard, but I've been blessed with the ability to help people look inside and discover that they already have the heart, the brains, and, most importantly, the courage to take control of their businesses, and ultimately, their lives. And it's a good bet that is everything you need to be successful, too. Well, *almost* everything.

As a business mentor I also have to help you do one other thing: use your heart, your brain, and your courage to create and execute a sound business plan.

Don't kid yourself. This journey will be every bit as tough as the one that Dorothy, Tin Man, Scarecrow, and Lion had to endure.

It also has the potential to be every bit as rewarding.

YOU ALREADY HAVE WHAT IT TAKES

While working in my own family business for more than 25 years, I was lucky enough to meet some of the top contractors from all around the country, and I'm fortunate now to work and talk with many more of you.

Here's what I can tell you—we as contractors already have what we need when it comes to heart, brains, and courage.

I know you have all the heart you'll ever need because there is no way you would have started this journey without a lot of heart. You're passionate about what you do, and your intentions to help others be warm, cool, safe, and comfortable are pure heart.

You also have all the brainpower you'll ever need. As a contractor, you had to study to get licensed and even now must study constantly to stay up on all the products out there that are constantly changing.

Finally, I know you have courage. It took a load of guts to venture off in your own business when you could have stayed at your old job, received a steady paycheck, and slept well at night. You're nothing but courageous.

So why aren't you as successful as you'd like to be?

Before success comes, you have to "see" it first, long before you can ever reach it. You have to decide what success means to you.

For Dorothy and friends, success meant different things (home, heart, brain, or courage), but their common goal was finding the Wizard of Oz. What does success mean to you and what does it look like? What is your end game? What goals will you need to set and achieve to get there?

Once you've got that pictured, the next step is to create and follow a well-designed plan—a yellow brick road—to make sure you're heading in the right direction.

Along this road there will be many challenges, and you will need to apply your heart, your brain, and your courage to execute your plan and reach your destination. Remember, getting to meet the wizard was only part of the journey they had to endure to get what they wanted! They also had to struggle to know themselves and examine their preconceived notions about others.

RECOVERING YOUR HEART

Maybe you're like Tin Man. Burnt out and feeling the passion for the work slipping away. At war with customers and employees, instead of seeing them as allies in your journey.

To regain your heart, your passion, you need to stop thinking about what you're not getting and start being thankful for all you have. Think about those who have entrusted their wellbeing to you—your customers and employees. They recognize you for the heart you have and have chosen to align themselves with you. Reclaim your heart by first being thankful that your customers and your employees have chosen you. Aspire to be that person they see.

Another way to recover your heart and your passion is to hire new young staff based on willingness and a positive attitude, and provide them with the training that will build their skills the right way. Their can-do attitude will reignite your own passion as you move toward inspiring them to be their best and rekindle the fire that drove you when you first started out on your own.

Add some *fun* to your day. (Remember fun?) Create some games and contests for yourself and your employees and let the positive competitive juices flow. Celebrate their wins and coach them when they fail so they can win the next time. The important thing is to work *and* play together as a team.

Finally, take a few minutes to look in the mirror and let yourself see the passionate person you once were. Inspire others by inspiring yourself first.

RECLAIMING YOUR BRAIN

When it comes to your brain, maybe you're like Scarecrow, in total contractor overload. You read constantly but don't know what to do with the information you collect. You know you should have a business plan but have no idea where to begin and so you're winging it.

Or, maybe you do have a new business plan but you change it just about every week. The result is too many different plans at work, and staff who are disenchanted and stalemated because they've been trained to wait and watch you change your mind. Like England's weather, they think, "If you don't like the plan or decision, wait a minute . . . it'll change." Having too many differing plans at work from too many bosses is like asking the Scarecrow for directions and having him point in opposite directions at the same time!

Your brain can easily get overloaded with too many things to remember and too much knowledge coming at you. It must be sifted and filtered to make sure it fits. Your yellow brick road needs to be paved with systems that are repeatable and in writing. Get your team on board with your plan by inviting them to fine-tune the process with you. Let them download all the good knowledge locked up in your brain, so they can help you and your brainpower is freed up to work on your business.

Whatever you do, don't follow the path of mismatching business systems or you'll end up building a Frankenstein. And you can't get to your Emerald City with a Frankenstein. Talk about scary!

REGAINING YOUR COURAGE

When it comes to courage, maybe you're more like Lion. You've created a well-designed plan to get the success you want, but you're afraid to implement it. What's holding you back? Is there a lack of commitment causing you to procrastinate? It takes courage to attack your areas of weakness.

It can be scary to create a business plan with measurable goals and objective tracking and to implement a set of standards and hold people accountable to them. And it's challenging to create and execute a well-tuned marketing plan. Learning to trust and empower others, and becoming great at recruiting, hiring, orienting, training, and retaining staff, is new territory for most and rife with the unknown. Add learning the basics of business finance and how to become better at selling, and you may want to run for the hills.

You're afraid because you think you have to do everything at once, and the reality is you can't, and more importantly, you shouldn't. Because, as you've discovered, it's too scary!

To recover your courage, you need to regain control of how you spend your time, and to do that you need to drastically narrow down the list of all the things you think you need to spend time doing. You need to establish a process that will enable you and your staff to chip away consistently at a few projects and habits that will add the most value to your company or solve its biggest problems.

You may be more or less like Tin Man, Scarecrow, or Lion, but to create a business, and ultimately a life with less stress and more success, you'll need to apply all the heart, brains, and courage you've got.

Good thing you've got a lot. Use them to follow the seven powers, and just like the ruby slippers, they will get you exactly where you want to go.

THE 7 POWERS—JIM CRINITI

I came from the military and so when I went into our family business after the service, I really missed that level of structure and organization. I knew that structure and systems would make our business better, but the problem was even though I'd operated successfully in a structured environment, I had no idea how to create one.

My brothers and dad and I were all working hard in the business, 12 to 14 hours a day, until one day I realized that it had grown to the point where we didn't really have control of it anymore, and we needed help. That's when I found Al. He taught us the seven powers and helped us use them to create the structured and organized environment I had always envisioned for Zoom, and it has made all the difference.

—*Jim Criniti, President, Zoom Drain,*
Philadelphia, Pennsylvania

About the Author

AL LEVI is a business consultant, teacher, author, *and* a former contractor who worked for 25 years in every aspect of his family's Long Island-based HVAC/plumbing business. The systems Al put in place enabled him to sell his share of the business to his brothers and retire before he was 50.

Al now helps other contractors learn to run their businesses with less stress and more success through consultations, workshops, webinars, and his long-running column in *Plumbing & Mechanical* magazine. An avid golfer who also does yoga and tai chi, Al resides in Scottsdale, Arizona, with his wife, Natalie.

For more information about Al's programs, please send an email to info@appleseedbusiness.com or visit www.appleseedbusiness.com.

Acknowledgments

I want to thank Helena Bouchez of www.ExecutiveWords.com for helping me move this mountain of materials from my own life's work as a contractor and consultant to contractors of all trades and company sizes into a tight, well-written business book. But Helena did more than that. She distilled my vast library of business blogs, articles, templates, forms, programs, and one-to-one client interviews into a wonderful business storybook, as she promised she would do. And in my humble literary opinion, Helena did it in a way that not many editors could ever have done. She was true to her commitment to me that the book would sound like you (the reader) and I were having a conversation over a cup of coffee. Helena, I'm forever grateful!

I also want you to know that Dan Holohan www.HeatingHelp.com has been a good friend and great mentor to me over the years, and his pearls of wisdom appear frequently in my columns for *Plumbing & Mechanical* magazine. In fact, if not for Dan, I'd probably still be out there turning wrenches late into the night. Dan cared enough to hold up the truth mirror so I could see that how I was helping to operate my family's contracting business was not good for me or the company in the long run—and then he showed me a better way. Dan was also the first one to encourage me to rework my columns, posts, and teaching materials into other formats, which inspired me to write *The 7-Power Contractor*. Dan, for all of this and more, I thank you.

Finally, Ellen Rohr of www.EllenRohr.com makes me not just a better business coach but also a better person. She's a bundle of positive energy. Ellen makes what contractors must learn about what I call Financial Power fun. Did I say financial and fun in the same sentence? Yes, yes, I did. Ellen has worked with many of my clients mentioned in this book and a whole lot more who we didn't have space to mention. Those clients have told me she helped them understand, as contractors, that one of best tools to have in their business toolbox is the skill to do budgeting and to run their company in real time, with the financial basics that they typically don't teach you in school. Ellen is also a business matchmaker, and the one who introduced me to Helena Bouchez, editor of *The 7-Power Contractor*. Ellen, I'm forever grateful for all you do for me as a business ally, and even more so as a friend.

Need More Guidance?

This book is intended as a how-to guide for creating a business you can run with less stress and more success, essentially, how you can *become* a 7-Power Contractor. We encourage you to dive in and start investing the time and effort needed to work through Planning Power as soon as possible!

For those of you who want to realize the benefits of this system faster, or simply don't want to undertake it alone, help is available. To find out more, we invite you to schedule a free 30-minute consulting call with Al Levi by visiting www.appleseedbusiness.com/free-consult.

Also under development: *The 7-Power Contractor* webinar and seminar series. By registering to download the bonus materials on the next page, you will automatically be notified when these programs become available.

We look forward to hearing how these seven power concepts have helped you begin to run your business with less stress and more success.

The time to begin is now. You, your family, and your customers will be so glad you did.

Bonus Materials

To access and download bonus materials associated with this book, visit www.appleseedbusiness.com/7PC and enter your name and the password "Power!" (without the quotes). Bonus materials include:

1. Example of Top Five Whiteboards (PDF)
2. Sample Organizational Chart (PDF)
3. Sample Operations Manual Section (PDF)
4. Fast Budget Excel Worksheet (Excel)
5. Marketing Allocation Worksheet (Excel)
6. Sample Marketing Calendar (PDF)

In addition to these tools, Ellen Rohr's excellent financial materials can be obtained at www.ellenrohr.com.

More information about Al Levi and Appleseed Business, Inc. can be found at www.appleseedbusiness.com.

Made in the USA
Middletown, DE
09 October 2023

40317713R00086